♥HEAVEN SPEAKS♥

Intimate Revelations from
Illuminated Souls

HEAVEN SPEAKS

Intimate Revelations from Illuminated Souls

Volume One

Walter Cronkite * Michael Jackson *

Abraham Lincoln * Albert Einstein *

Amelia Earhart * Paul Newman *

Walt Disney * John Lennon

via Pamela Bloom and Carla Flack

DEDICATION

To Ken

who was the start of it all

To Robert and Barbara Young

for angel wings

&

To our heavenly "hosts"

for the privilege

CONTENTS

INTRODUCTION - Pamela

How do you come to a point in your life when you can sit down and talk to dead people?

And not just dead ones.

Famous ones. Celebrities. People of note.

But really, really dead ones.

The answer isn't easy. It's like asking Isaac Stern how he plays the violin. Or Sir Laurence Olivier how he acts.

Or Michael Jackson how he does the Moonwalk.

(Actually, in this book we did get to ask Michael about the Moonwalk. But you'll have to read his chapter to find out!)

Right now, we want to explain who we are and how we've come to present this book—a compilation of channeled interviews with notable (dead) souls of our time. If you're not up on these things, you might think it's a hoax. And you have every right to. Saying you can talk to dead people and have them talk back, particularly famous ones, could well be the biggest joke in the world.

We don't think it is. But to really explain who we are and how we do it will take a bit of explanation.

Both Carla, my co-author, and I have spent the majority of our adult lives involved in intuitive development. I have a deep background in meditation and have also pursued things like prayer, hypnosis and guided imagery—first to heal my own inner life and then to help others. I've been an interfaith minister, hospital chaplain and an intuitive counselor able to read deep soul patterns in clients. Throughout the years I've worked a lot with people who have had life-challenging illnesses, and my personal counseling work was dedicated to helping them free themselves to be healthier, happier, more loving and more creative.

Carla's background leans to the metaphysical arts (astrology, angels, tarot, numerology, shamanism, mediumship, past-life regression, etc.), but she is also an interfaith minister who is more interested in soul development and evolution than giving out the telephone number for someone's soul mate. She has been an intuitive counselor for thirty-seven years and continues to be amazed by the process.

One day, Carla and I met serendipitously in an AOL healing chat room. Except for one lovely fall weekend in New York, we have never spent physical time together, instead becoming the proverbial e-mail friends, capable of deeply felt exchanges precisely because of our clairvoyant abilities. Simply, we trusted each other's insights: there is nothing like feeling someone can look into the depths of your soul that creates a bond surpassing all triviality.

In the interim years, concurrent with my counseling work, I became a professional writer exploring many fields—travel journalism, spiritual books, fiction, advertising and marketing projects. From her home in Indiana, Carla helped found an internet intuitive counseling website, taught Angel and Tarot workshops and authored a book on Tarot. She even contributed to a two-book set of prayers I was editing for the publisher Guideposts.

Our long-distance friendship surged and waned until finally in 2009 we happily found each other again. As it is with deeply connected souls, it was as if we had never been apart. Compatible but different in our talents, we always had a deep feeling we would collaborate on something great.

Then one day, following the passing of the epic newscaster Walter Cronkite, the gentleman Carla was seeing made a casual joke: "Why doesn't somebody talk to him in heaven?" he said. "That would sure be some broadcast!"

When Carla told me the idea, we both laughed and said, "Well, why not?" In a playful mood we decided to try and see what would happen. We had no real plan. It was fun. It was play. It was free!

From the very first, though, we were **dumbstruck** at the depth that came flowing through. And that depth never wavered. It only grew. And we loved doing it. Soon we both had the distinct feeling that hundreds of souls were lining up to talk to us. It seemed to be as much a pleasure for "them" on the other side as it was for us.

Which is not to say that I, personally, did not have a few misgivings. I am a professional journalist, and I don't take "psychic sentiment" for granted. Many books of mine have been based on the accuracy of facts that can be easily proven. Also, as a meditator, I know how the mind can fool itself. I understand the power of ego to distort.

In fact, I could think of a million reasons not to pursue this work, not the least of which was my professional reputation. But I put them all aside, for one reason on which I'll blame Carla—because it's the very reason why I love her so much. In the intuitive realm, Carla is fearless. A risk-taker. The epitome of a maverick and pioneer.

And without her, this book would not have come to completion.

Talking to dead people all by yourself can be very lonely! So I'm not shy about saying that it has been Carla's winning companionship and collaboration that has made this book possible. Although most of our transmissions were done independently of each other, we did confer daily and share our discoveries. One thing we did not do, however, was read each other's transmissions if we were still working on the same subject. That is to say, if I was "interviewing" Michael Jackson (i.e., typing up the transmission as I received it), she wouldn't read the results until she had finished her own time with him. That way we didn't influence each other and our individual reportage retained its independent veracity.

Once, in the case of Walter Cronkite, we did channel the transmission orally with each other, using Skype. It was a great moment to make a fool of ourselves in front of the other, but that never happened. The work always proved itself to be true—and authentic.

Strangely enough, our transmissions remained distinct, yet compatible. Carla was more interested in the moments and conditions of a soul's passing and journey to the other side. I was more interested in lessons learned and spiritual truths gleaned. We were both interested in what the experience of Heaven—the after-death life—looks and feels like.

But the story of this book is not limited to the actual content of the interviews. The sensations, the synchronicities, the intuitions we experienced with our subjects may be as interesting for our readers as the interviews themselves; beyond our introductions for each subject, you'll find more of that kind of material in our Epilogues. And yet all that—the synchronicity of facts—is simply food for the rationale brain. The true impact of this work, we feel, will be felt in the soul.

One thing Carla and I would like you to understand before you read another word: both of us believe that whatever gift allows us to perform these transmissions are *natural abilities* that all of us have. Classic books like Gary Zukav's *The Seat of the Soul* and *You Are Psychic!* by Pete Sanders, a MIT-trained physicist, as well as myriad books by present-day mediums such as John Edward, Sylvia Browne and James van Praagh, all put forth the argument that Consciousness on a global level is about to break open, and who we really are—energetically, spiritually, interdimensionally—will soon become revealed to all of us.

Simply, we are more than who we think we are.

And we believe Heaven is about to open its truths to all of us—soon.

That's why we have the interest, the passion and the courage to act as what we term the "conscious mediums" of this work. We discovered—in the first moment of playfulness when we felt Walter coming through—that the process was one of the most natural we had ever engaged in. We don't go deeply into any trances. We don't roll our eyes up into our head (although a voice teacher did teach me once how to do that but it had absolutely no affect on my singing voice!). And we don't have funny voices come through.

Simply, after many years of intuitive development, both of us have developed the capacity to slightly shift our conscious attention, like tuning a radio channel, and hear/receive the transmissions that are coming through.

By "hear," Carla and I define the word differently. For myself, I seem to "hear" a stream-of-consciousness flow of thoughts in the very place in my awareness where I think my own thoughts; it's clear to me, however, that these are not my own thoughts. I can tell. They come too fast—and too eloquent—for me to be making it up. That I know.

For Carla, it comes in several ways—from short snippets or phrases to long, complete streams of information. To her, it's more "feeling" the words than hearing them. Sometimes it's like a running ticker tape of words imprinted across her forehead. The secret, she says, is getting "out of the way" and letting the words/thoughts/visions flow. But she also has wild, out-of-session experiences—images and visual impressions just pop up. She once e-mailed me to say Bob Hope had just showed up, swinging his golf club and saying he'd wait patiently for his turn at the mike. You just had to laugh.

Skeptics might say that this is just a bunch of creative malarkey. Maybe. That's a distinct possibility we sometimes entertain because we don't have an ego investment in any of this. Carla strongly feels, and I agree, that any intuitive work like this ALWAYS involves the filter of the medium. It's unavoidable. Even the work of Edgar Cayce, the classic unconscious medium of the last century who went into deep trance to do his spectacular work, was affected in some way by his personal focus.

That is to say, it *is* possible that our spiritual beliefs, our psychological understanding or lack of it, our capacity for language, our mood of the moment, etc., may all come into play in these interviews—in some way.

You decide.

But what Carla and I do stand by—when we step back and look at the quality of this material—is that the spiritual depth and psychological authenticity of the results cannot be dismissed. It is said that everybody becomes a little more evolved when they die—in fact, death may be the biggest personal growth factor any of us ever experience! And these interviews prove it. Maybe that's why these celebrities sound a great deal more profound, spiritually advanced and psychologically astute than they ever did when they were alive. Or, to be more accurate, more than they did AS WE KNEW THEM TO BE—publicly, historically.

There's just something about having a bigger perspective than one's small ego that tends to make us smarter. And that's what passing from the body seems to do for you.

So, we want to warn you: You are about to discover aspects of these well-known souls that you never, ever imagined.

And therein lies what we feel is the deepest value of *Heaven Speaks.*

In these interviews, truths have been spoken. Confessions revealed. Spiritual ideas pointed to and revered. Moreover, whatever Carla and I thought personally about these celebrities prior to this work, we have, through the experience of touching their souls, come to feel enormous love, reverence and respect for each and every one of them, as well as a deep appreciation for revealing to us the one truth that seems to underlie every page of communication in this book.

And that truth is:

Life is eternal. Love is immortal. And death is just a horizon.

And thank you, Carly Simon, for that wonderful sentiment— she who is the only dear celebrity mentioned in this book who is still gloriously alive with us on this planet! And thank God for that!

(Did we mention, everybody else is dead?!)

But talk about the synchronicities…when Heaven begins to speak…

As I sit in a coffee shop in Queens, New York, finishing up the first draft of this introduction, who should come onto the radio but…

Yes.

John Lennon. Singing…

"Imagine…imagine all the people…living life in peace…"

And so, we thank you, John (and yes, we plan to get the mike to you soon!). That is EXACTLY the message *Heaven Speaks* on every page.

The Plan that has been addressed over and over again. The one Abe Lincoln first brought to our attention. The one Walter spoke of. The one Michael is still yearning for.

Imagine…the world…in peace.

From Heaven to our ears…

Just imagine…

So stick around. Stay tuned with us. And hang on for the ride of your life.

Because…

Heaven is speaking…

And in the immortal words of Walter Cronkite, our first beloved interviewee (for whom we shall always hold a burning candle):

"…and that's the way it is."

With love, wonder and Oneness,

--Pamela Bloom
Queens, New York

INTRODUCTION – Carla

To say this has been an interesting way to write a book would be an understatement. Pamela wrote the majority of the introduction while sitting in a coffee shop. Now that we've completed the book, I'm writing this part of the introduction after the fact and still don't know where to start.

When this project began, we had been talking about collaborating on a book, a play or a movie for about four months. At the time, we had **no** idea what was just around the corner.

As we waited to zero in on a stimulating project, we were both reading Joe Vitale's *Zero Limits* and knew that inspiration could strike at any moment. And it's true! A simple statement from a friend—at the same time I was writing an e-mail to Pamela—is all it took! One moment of inspiration (at the perfect moment in time) and we were on our way.

Although I could literally **feel** the celebrities lining up to talk to us, we let them take us in whatever direction they wanted to go. The conversations with each personality felt so anchored, enlightening and sincere.

It was surprising to feel the presence of Abraham Lincoln among the more contemporary figures, but we didn't edit the "line-up"; we just followed their lead. He seemed to just jump in and take his place in a matter-of-fact kind of way.

The "crossing-over" experience has always been fascinating to me for some reason. The near-death accounts I've read usually involved the spirit traveling through a tunnel toward a bright light. I hadn't even considered that there could be a multitude of sights, sounds and feelings on that journey.

When the first experience from Walter Cronkite came through, I was hooked! There was so much more than a static journey through a tunnel toward a bright light. The travels were holographic and individual. Although the destination is the same, the experience seems to be as personal and varied as the personalities taking the trip—without exception.

I do believe that we are closer to the "other side" now than we have ever been. I think the higher dimensions are open to our curiosity, wonder and development. All we have to do is allow our consciousness to expand to its highest potential and let the information flow.

You will see that we've chronicled the interview dates not only so we could keep track of the progression but because you may enjoy following how the book developed.

This project has confirmed to me, once again, that we are unlimited beings. The only limits to what we can achieve (or "establish," as John Lennon says) are the limits we impose upon ourselves.

Trust in the magic.

With Love and our greatest respect and gratitude,

--Carla Flack
Lafayette, Indiana

WALTER CRONKITE

Journalist/Broadcaster/TV News Anchorman

Born: November 4, 1916

Died: July 17, 2009

First Transmission: September 27, 2009

Pamela

Walter Cronkite was our first transmission and perhaps our most light-hearted approach since we both entered the project with absolutely no expectations. Over a series of days, after someone Carla knew joked about the possibility of interviewing Walter Cronkite posthumously, the quintessential anchorman seemed to flip in and out of our awareness; once he got started, though, he proved himself to be clear-headed and determined to communicate in an exceedingly smooth fashion.

From the start, Carla and I seemed to fall organically into patterns that we would maintain for the rest of the book: We contacted each subject separately, typing the results as we received them, with Carla gravitating toward asking about the moment of passing over, and I, about life lessons. In the middle of our connection with Walter, as we were still experimenting, we decided to use Skype to see if I could orally channel Walter while Carla posed the questions. What came through was equally clear; the big surprise was to feel my voice drop in depth, matched by an uncommon (for me!) sense of authority and presence—just as we knew Walter to be in life. In fact I felt him as very grandfatherly.

Still, I was surprised when Walter steered the discussion around to aging; it turned out he actually had a great deal to say how the repercussions of aging are psychologically and socially devastating our society. But the overwhelming feeling I had from his sessions was the enormous gratitude he felt for the richness of his past life and for the love that he had experienced both in his marriage and in relationship; in fact, despite all his honors, he had come to feel that love was the most important aspect of life that lingers on into the next realm.

On a funny note, both Carla and I had the strong impression that Walter was vying to be "the producer" of this work; right after I texted that impression to Carla from my phone, I walked into a Barnes & Noble, and there, on the very first table, at the right-hand corner, was a book that immediately caught my eye—a new novel with the very strange title of Top Producer. *The coincidence was, well, just too coincidental! And was Walter forever the producer—even advising me how to conduct an interview! It did feel good, however, to know that such a revered journalist as Walter Cronkite would be by our side!*

Pamela
September 26, 2009

Hi, Walter. At your command. Is there something you would like to share about what you learned on earth? [In my own mind I am thinking about how integrity must have been an important part of his life; he took up these thoughts and continued them.]

Walter: You are correct. Integrity is part and parcel of life. Without integrity there is no real transmission of knowledge because integrity allows for receptivity. We listen to those we respect. Respect comes about from something deep within. I have thought about this a lot in my life, particularly when I was involved in sticky situations. In the newsroom. On the field. You can buy information. You can report it objectively. But what real objectivity is, well, I am learning that here.

Perhaps this is the biggest difference. What is integrity on your plane is not the same here. And yet there is a connection. But think of colors. A flat pink versus a multi-hued maroon with varying shades and vicissitudes. This is what integrity is on this plane. There is no getting attached to one form. Attachment equals solidification and then you lose the flow here.

There was a bit of stodginess about my sense of integrity on earth. A little bit black and white. You want that in a newscaster, however. An impartiality with an undercurrent of compassion. You don't want to feel the person who brings you the news is a death-defying risk-taker (because you KNOW that person would fudge with the truth) nor do you want someone who doesn't have enough balls to bear and withstand the truth. But I thought while on earth that you had to be stoic, you had to be a man fifties-style; you had to show you wouldn't buckle, whether a nuclear blast hit Russia or your grandchild was born dead. The world didn't want to see a sissy man as anchor.

It may seem strange to you, but I have begun to rethink these assumptions. In fact much of heaven here is a rethinking of any belief you may have held dear. A kind of Thoughts Anonymous realm, a Beliefs Anonymous realm. We learn how much of our identity we funneled into those thoughts and beliefs that we hold so dear, consciously and unconsciously, and our guides here help us learn how to transmute them into light. It's an honest day's work. I actually enjoy it because one feels the lightness that suffuses the being at the end of the day (although there are no days or time as such, as you know it) but at the end of a naturally concluding episode, might I say. Whereas, in life you'd have to end the day with a hard drink because thoughts had solidified, hardened into emotions. The weight of all that!

Now we actually have processes where we get lighter and lighter. A constant diet of the soul, so to speak. For those who like to accumulate things, this might be frightening or uncomfortable, but most of us get along because it is as if there is a perfect-weather vibration that goes on around us. It vibrates with perfection so as we become lighter, we ease—melt, perhaps you could say—into this vibration. And it makes it all easier.

--Walter Cronkite

Carla

The first information I received from Walter was so powerful. Wow!

The feel of his passing was so calm and grounded— centered with a sense of authority and yet an uncomplicated willingness to share and divulge. All this came with an overlay of such peace. The transmission just flowed so easily and spontaneously.

The first contact brought a big smile to my face—injected as it was with a sense of humor and the personal reference to his physical personality's passion during his lifetime. I could feel his centered excitement but also the extreme gratitude running through it.

Walter traveled over, not with a fast whoosh of energy through a tunnel, but rather with a slow, swirling, relaxed energy of sound and color. Through his description, I could feel the inadequacy of descriptive words. I didn't feel he was frustrated with his inability to describe it; it was more like he was surprised, taken aback or in wonder of how awe-inspiring the experience was to him. This is a man who used words in an eloquent way. His business was to report and explain things in understandable language. And yet, here he was—in a realm where words and expressions were now inadequate.

I could very much feel him re-experiencing the whole thing— or I could say—I was watching him re-experience the occurrence.

Carla
September 26, 2009

Walter, Tell me about crossing over. I want to know the feelings, the sights, the sounds—all of it.

Walter: That's one small step for man (chuckling).

Sorry. I couldn't help reflecting on my life's love, passion and inspiration of space and time outside the Earth's atmosphere. That subject always made me sit forward in my chair with the body trying to immerse itself in the wonder and amazement of it all. Made me feel like a child again.

Would it be interesting for people to know that I passed over three hours before I was officially pronounced dead? There was a "lapse" time in my departure—and I know it doesn't happen that way with everyone—but, in my case, my spirit must have had some incomplete issues (some call it energy) to finish before completely crossing over. Interesting trip that was!

In reality, I could have left the physical plane two years before I passed but I got a reprieve of sorts that brought bonus time with my awe-inspiring family and friends. This actually happens quite often. More now than in the past. It wasn't because I was afraid to die. It was because of my interest in LIFE. Like reading a book and not putting it down until you see the words "The End".

My soul's departure was slow and easy. Yes. There was a "tunnel" experience but it was not the kind that "whooshed" me toward the Light. It was more a slow and easy spiral filled with music and color that is indescribable on the physical plane. I passed through the wonderment of it all, literally absorbing it into my being. The colors so pure and clear and cleansing. The music so entrancing and hypnotic. One has to experience it to even attempt to put words to it.

Through that passage, I experienced a life review and actually so enjoyed the feeling that I believe it's why the energy transition seemed slow, effortless and peaceful to me. It's actually pretty amazing, that passage. The reality of it is very impressive. One would expect to transition or relive the major events of one's life, but I was amazed at how the little things so grasped my attention. The first time I stopped in my tracks to look for the bird I heard singing. The small breath taken in an intimate moment. The wonder of the wind or cold or rain so taken for granted in the physical. It's actually a very humbling experience.

At the end of the tunnel were numerous spirits or souls who had been waiting to start the celebration party of my arrival. My first attraction was, of course, to Betsy [*his deceased wife*]. It was like being a teenager again—that swirl of inner knowing and connection. Much like receiving a blue ribbon in some ways. Knowing that you, together, had completed some sort of predetermined or predestined goal that was a personal and collective accomplishment.

There were many family members, friends and others that some would consider celebrities, scientists, statesmen, etc. And others that I had no personal recollection of, but through what I will call spirit recognition, I "knew" them immediately. Soldiers I had walked by while reporting from Vietnam. Engineers in the space program who had been in "subconsciously" visual range. "Ordinary" people I'd passed by on the street or while riding in a car. The scope of it all is almost overwhelming when you truly feel the number of lives we connect with, and to, on an ongoing basis.

The truth is, I didn't feel much different than I did on the physical plane with the exception of how large and all-encompassing it is. An existence without boundaries. A knowing without questioning. A sense of peace without interruption.

I thought I had a hand on the pulse of the world from my anchor desk. But it was nothing compared to the 360-degree bird's eye view that I have now.

And that's the way it is. . . .

--Walter Cronkite

Pamela
September 28, 2009

Walter, would you like to continue speaking about what life is like there?

Walter: You are asking me about things…I have to go back into that state of mind where I had those opinions because in this realm they are beginning to fade fast.

It is as if there are two of me, one here, the other one a thought bubble with enormous opinions having to do with "that" life. It is a switch to go back and forth between the two. If you ask me, the one that seems more authentic is this one [*the one without opinions*]. The one that seems more energetic, earth-wise speaking, is the opinionated one. When I do go into that bubble of thought-opinions, there is a kind of downgrading of my soul pattern, so to speak. I come back a bit exhausted. This is teaching me that perhaps those kind of thoughts [*opinions*] are not so beneficial, but I would be willing to cooperate for a while to see if it goes anywhere or is helpful to you. Again, those [*opinion-like*] thoughts seem permeated with ego, and like a diet of hamburgers and fries, something you tend to want to leave behind when you decide to live a "healthy" [*heavenly*] lifestyle. That's not to say they still don't have their hold on you and sometimes you want to indulge but in general you stay away. That's my feeling about running on about those beliefs and opinions.

Please don't tax me to the point that the soul becomes bloated from mind-fatigue!

Walter, is there a bigger picture about life that you would like to talk about?

Walter: It's a question of whether you stand back or throw yourself in—into life. And this is really the dilemma that people on earth have. Stand back and watch or throw yourself in. I had the very great opportunity to do both in my career—I am referring to times when I was in the field as a newscaster and later as I sat as an anchor, which I'd describe as a bit more standing back and watching.

Some of this has to do with age. There are times when throwing yourself into life is really where it's at. And at other times, as you age there is a natural sitting back. I was very fortunate in my career that both of those phases could be embraced in my profession and I have a great deal of gratitude for that.

As I look from this perspective I see a great problem with people getting older and losing their place in life and losing the passion for being *in* life because they have lost the energy to throw themselves in. And they don't see the rich opportunity to stand back and still be active in the world.

This is going to be even more a problem as all the baby boomers age.

And so, I was considered an elder statesmen. In fact as I got older, that kind of mantle, that cloak of respect grew heavier and heavier. And so, even though I may have felt a longing to be younger, to be more involved, at least my aging was surrounded by the kind of respect and honor that most people can only imagine and long for.

In this way I feel so grateful because I have seen many people arrive here in heaven with a kind of lackluster or depressed attitude for the possibilities of life because the end of their life became so...diminished...and so burdened by illness and disease and sometimes abandonment by the family, so that these emotional patterns became heavier than anything else in life, heavier than the positive moments in their lives.

As strange as this may seem—and this may surprise Carla!—I have become very interested in how I can help people age and pass over with a more accomplished feeling in their hearts so that they can continue to evolve at a quicker pace than having to take time when they first arrive to heal the last part of their lives.

Again, I was very fortunate, even after my wife passed, to find other companionship, even though it created some problems with my children and family—a kind of female companionship that kept me youthful in my heart, and I so appreciate whatever blessings in my life brought love to my life throughout its days. I also saw many of my colleagues have this kind of diminishment of soul because they put so much into work and did not have the kind of support and love that I did at home.

So another message I want to leave people: no amount of accomplishment from the physical level equals the value of love, being loved and loving, being cherished and cherishing. That's what the real accomplishment is. That's what the real news is. Nothing that we rarely put on the news—but rather, *these* moments—the moments of love— which are the moments that sustain you over here.

Everything else dissolves.

And so that is what I would like to leave you with. Make your heart activity your news and broadcast from there. It's not outside of you. And that is one thing I also learned. My life was dedicated to reporting what took place outside of me. And the truth was, what was most important was this life inside. That's what in every life should be reported. When we took that attitude in our news story, to find the inner story, to find the heart story, we were always successful. It wasn't about numbers. It wasn't about how many people got killed, how much money was made, how many houses destroyed; it was the human story of sacrifice and courage and love and devotion and fearlessness—this is what the real news is about and what evolves this society. Not celebritydom. Not controversy.

And it is my prayer that I remember this on the next go-round.

Carla: *And that's the way it is!*

Pamela: *Thank you, Walter!*

Carla
September 28, 2009

Walter, is there anything else you'd like to convey or discuss at this time? I have a lingering feeling that something is missing or incomplete. I keep hearing the words "accuracy" and "depth."

Walter: There's nothing pressing from my point of view but there evidently is from your perspective. So I'll go on....

Opinions don't really matter much. Oh, you think they do and opinions do shape your world to some extent. But a singular person's opinion doesn't matter until it connects with other like-opinionated people. I had opinions about newsworthy items and there's an art to objective journalism that may now be extinct. I guess in some ways you could call me a dinosaur.

When an opinion integrates into a news story, the story loses some integrity and turns more toward entertainment than reporting the news. Don't exchange opinion with emotion. You can wed news and emotion in a genuine, accurate way. Emotion is part of the human condition and it's a blessing.

You observed genuine emotion in my broadcast of Kennedy's assassination. The emotion I felt then was as much sadness for humanity as it was for the loss of the man himself. We truly understood that time in history to be a tipping point toward the loss of innocence. And that innocence will never be regained in its true form and original condition. And yet, each such instance is a clue to the next opportunity to change the world for the better.

It's the human way to continue to repeat history in one form or another. As humans, we learn by repetition or experience. Usually we learn through a combination of both by repeating an experience. The question is, how will you use recognized experience to create a better future?

Since I mentioned passing by a soldier in Vietnam above, let's take a look at that. The Vietnam War. What an opportunity we had to recognize a rational way to end conflict of any kind.

In any conflict or disagreement, there is always a way to find the balance point or negotiate a win/win conclusion—with respect—for honorable people. It's a choice of objective thought and action. It's finding a way to blend personal conscience and a nation's conscience for the betterment of all concerned.

Which brings us back to the beginning of this session. Opinions and objectivity.

When personal opinions integrate into any action, there is a **loss of integrity.**

Any good news story has a beginning and an ending. Through the process you will find the beginning usually circles around to meet the ending.

A completion. A beginning. An end. A complete circle of life.

* * *

Pamela
September 29, 2009

Walter, anything more to say on lessons learned, or what it's like to be there?

Walter: I do have something to say about interviewing and maybe this is where I can help you. It helps to target the individual. It's good, right, to have an overall approach, particularly in a book where you are looking for some consistency. But to make interviews fly, and capture a spontaneous reportage from the interviewee, you need to catch him or her off guard—say, at the end of an expected list of questions, you drop that killer one in. That's when you have their attention, you have their trust, their openness, and especially their vulnerability. Interviewers have to be open to themselves first and foremost. Many people are like shut clams but it is up to the interviewer to make it happen, to crack open the shell.

So some suggestions. Feel free to interrogate me. Even though I said the other night to not burden me with questions, you need to have some specific triggers to get me going; otherwise we don't have a clue what to draw on. Especially since this is a book with a format and other "condensees." I enjoyed making word plays when I was young (that is, on earth) but didn't have the scope or platform on air to really run with it. Now I am beside myself with these kinds of jokes and word play. William Safire [*a famous linguist columnist of the* New York Times *who died recently*] has joined us and it is a pleasure to discuss linguistics with him. You see, this kind of passion and knowledge still stays with us, at least at this point. Not language per se, as there is no actual speech, but the play of meaning, the play of language; here it is also the play of images that have meaning. With agile minds, it is a bit like playing volleyball with concepts. There is that kind of amusement here, that kind of delight in spontaneous play.

My life on earth was quite rigid, as I have said earlier. Fifties-style Marlboro man. You didn't want to write the word "Marlboro," as I understand that I don't come off like a cowboy, but that kind of stoicism was expected of this generation. It tied us up into all sorts of emotional patterns that were not good for relationships, not expressing tears, etc. That's why that one tear I had when JFK was assassinated was so powerful. That one tear existed in a cultural vacuum of tears for men of that generation. If I had cried a bucket, or put my head down on the desk and wailed, it wouldn't have had the same effect.

But one tear—moved a nation. One tear moved a world.

And it wasn't planned obviously. That taking off of my glasses was a moment of reverence, when I stopped being the newscaster for a moment, and began being a man, a member of the society, for a moment feeling what everybody else was feeling. Like others, I felt the assassination like a dagger in the heart, the awesomeness of it. The sense life would never be the same. We had the same feeling after 911. The awesomeness, the scope. As a newsman, how I would have wanted to be at a desk during that day and days to follow. It was my kind of story. It was the story of the century. It happened on our lands, not in Normandy, not in Vietnam, in rainforests on the other side of the world. It happened amongst us.

Interesting perhaps to you: They showed some of my old reels to me here. Like on a movie screen. I was to watch and give my feedback. At first I saw my younger self in combat clothes, at the anchor desk, etc., in all sorts of positions, and I remembered those moments; maybe there was some critical thoughts, oh, I should have done this or that, but the guidance here pointed out that the MIND is very much like these newsreels. Events, emotions, reactions playing out on a screen, like one of my newsreels on the TV screen. In that moment, the reel is a reel, not REAL. It is just a moving picture. And they are trying to teach me that the MIND, the essence and nature of the mind, is just like a REEL, and not REAL.

I love the play of words there, as I said before. REEL, NOT REAL—it has become almost a slogan for me. It is a shocking thing to realize and I am slowly coming to fashion it. This "fashioning" is not like another thought, but a deep-seated insight, a gut feeling that this is true, beyond my mind. I am beginning to trust that but I see it is a process. When it happens it will be all at once; until then it seems to take place in steps, on a journey.

One thing important: I, we, the friends here, the cronies, the colleagues—are all surrounded by love. There is no mistaking that. So it is relatively easy to learn these truths. It is not like a harsh disciplinary school but an oceanic field where we are held and supported. This learning is organic, easy, we love to learn. No tests except your own being speaking back to you loud and clear.

And that's the way it is!

--Walter Cronkite

"One tear moved a nation . . ."

MICHAEL JACKSON

World-Class Entertainer/Singer/Dancer/Songwriter

Born: August 29, 1958

Died: June 25, 2009

First Transmission: September 27, 2009

Pamela

By this time, the Universe knows of the tragic and untimely death of Michael Jackson. His body may have been stilled but not his spirit. Once he came on board (second in line after Walter Cronkite), Michael fast proved himself to be a very creative but impatient interviewee. Let's just say, he was dying to talk!

He initially came to me soon after I finished my first transmission from Walter; later in the same day, Carla picked up the trail but had a series of very intriguing obstacles before she and Michael could "sit down" to talk.

The wait seemed to make Michael very impatient and he nudged her all day long—while she was cleaning her pool, running errands, etc. When she finally did sit down, pen in hand, unexpected visitors would arrive, etc. Meanwhile, during that same afternoon as he was transmitting some information to me about his passing, I could actually feel him tapping his feet impatiently. He wanted Carla's attention! Finally, he received it, with the results below—a full-blown description of his passing into his new state of consciousness.

In my transmissions with Michael (which went on intermittently for weeks), I was struck by his honesty and vulnerability as well as his immense understanding and eloquence about the energy of music. I felt he could break into song at any minute, and he even did once, but it was not showmanship; it was a reflection of how much music infuses his soul, whether he has a body or not. He understands music, beyond notes, beyond words. Michael Jackson was, and still is, Music!

Pamela
September 27, 2009

Michael, do you have anything to share with us about your life on earth and the beyond?

Michael: When all is said and done I could be seen as a saint. It is the human quality that sneaks in and disturbs the momentum of the spirit, which was felt to want to launch out like a bullet. When I had that feeling of soul explosion, that's where I lived. It's like orgasm, better than that for me. Better than the personal. I never really found that [*the satisfaction of personal sexual relationships*] because it was too up close and the human got in the way. All my troubles inside me were on the personal realm. But the soul waited to explode on stage.

I also loved my children very much. It's where I could start from scratch and they didn't have to know the MJ everyone else had grown up with and heaped so many expectations on. I could start over, so to speak, and form their opinions just from the start, from zero ground.

The soul wanted to be like a bullet, a projectile that exploded before the world, before millions, before billions. There's nothing left when that happens, so it's hard to regroup afterwards. That's why you need help. Whether it's drugs or people or whatever. There is not an organizing principle left and you need to rely on others. It would explode the brain, whatever brain is left.

Most people don't understand what a performer gives of himself, the end, the last vestiges. It's a sacrifice and a duty.

Listen, music is in the blood. It's in the bones. It's in the way we breathe, the way we walk down the street. When you have that feeling of rhythm in you, you see it everywhere. There's no need to look for inspiration, it's right in front of you. The way a woman's hips sway, the way an old man hobbles. The way a car swerves around a curb. Whoosh, it's in your body and you express it. All those movements on stage come from life pouring through me. I don't think about it. I don't know how it happens and yet on some level I do know how it happens but it doesn't matter. I just let it happen. Whoosh and there comes another dance step, another curve in the voice. I open and it comes rushing through me. That's the gift. That's the grace. Nobody can give that to you, nobody can take that away from you, once you have it.

You *can* get so down, though, that you don't care. There were big holes of sadness in my life. I don't want to go into that now. I don't want to name names because it could get you in trouble and from this side it doesn't really matter. The hole is in you. Everyone has them and the point is to heal them. I see the nature of that now, why it works out that way. We are to open to the healing that is here. It's there too [*meaning, on earth*] but it's hard to see. It's right there walking among you, but it's like invisible smoke. Sometimes you can smell it, like a gas leak; other times it is around you like an invisible cloak. That's where faith comes in.

Don't knock people with faith. It's the doorway into the unseen. Faith propels you forward. Faith to hit the target; just to eye that target propels you forward. Someone leaping over a hurdle has FAITH that he will accomplish it. Yeah for faith!

Faith gives you comfort inside. Sometimes I'd have so many things, thoughts, bubbling over, foaming inside me, and I wouldn't know what to do. Faith would sustain me, faith would calm them down. I'd get my head on straight, but sometimes it wasn't enough. That's why I had to take the sleeping pills and all the other stuff to calm down this storm inside. This storm just wanted to come out, be heard, scream, manifest, do its thing. On stage it was fine. But it was too big to be contained and constantly tormented me. Even while I was loving my children.

I am beginning to see the light, so goes the song. [*"I am beginning to see the light"—he sings it in his special rhythm and begins to soft-shoe it. And then he laughs very softly, in his high, MJ girlish laugh.*]

Wow, took you a long time to write that and now it's over. That's the difference here; emotions rise, fall, but no stain, no holding, no lag time. It's beautiful in that way, music all the time. By music I mean this rhythm of life, these cadences of rise and fall but no stain, no holding on or holding back. Just rhythm of life. I am groovin'. I'm groovin', for sure.

I think this is enough for now to show you you can do this. It's the rhythm of life that will help you do it. The rhythm between us. Both hearing the same music. We can do it.

--MJ

Pamela
September 29, 2009

Michael, what was your passing like?

Michael: I had not slept all night and was frantic to get rest. I kept urging the doctor to give me more [*medicine or drugs to sleep*]. Finally he gave in. I slipped into a deep sleep, as if into mud. That's what it felt like, like I was steeped in mud, then sinking like quicksand falling down a shaft of light. As if I was falling down a well. Initial panic, then a sense of floating, flying. I was able to right myself up and then fell feet first. When I looked about I was out of the body and I saw the body being attended to by the doctor and some of my children frantically running about. I saw the ride to the hospital and the various attendants pumping on my chest.

General mayhem, at the same time the calm of professionals. In myself there was a great calm. I watched fascinated, saying, This is it. This is it. At least it didn't have to be painful.

In the hospital, it seems two angel guides came in to escort me on. They took me by the arm lovingly but I didn't want to go at first. I wanted to watch. It was something to view the body from this vantage point, this thing which had propelled my career now stilled. But it wasn't me. I was looking at something I had identified as me, had hated as me, had nudged and punished as me, had danced and loved through as me, but it wasn't me. That was a shock in some way, though I knew in the innermost that it wasn't me. I had known this always. I knew I was spirit. I just couldn't reconcile all the factors together that come with living a life.

***

Carla

When it was time to turn my attention to Michael, strange interferences started creeping in.

As much as I tried to "go there," my normal life seemed to step in and continually delay things. Unexpected visitors. My "real" job. Unplanned errands.

I found myself writing a sentence or paragraph at a time over the next day and a half. Michael indeed felt like he was tapping his foot, just waiting for me to take the time to listen.

His energy was quite different from Walter's. As Pamela said, he felt vulnerable and sincere. And I've got the feeling that he is far from done. I think he will be sticking around for awhile with some articulate and provocative things to pass along.

Carla
September 30, 2009

Michael, tell me about crossing over. The feelings. The sights. The sounds. . .all of it.

Michael: I crossed so peacefully. Without even knowing it.

It felt like being in a state of animated suspension, which is exactly what it was. That state of animated suspension didn't leave space for much differential between being in physical form or in spirit form.

So in essence it was a quiet, cordial, smooth, almost indistinguishable passing from one dimension to another, and yet, there was an energetic exchange that was notable.

Yes. There was a tunnel.

But it was not a long, dark tunnel where I was traveling to a source of light destination. It was a tunnel that was filled with light and music and harmony and was like surfing on a wonderful symphony of sound. Made me feel like dancing!

I was greeted at the tunnel-of-music's end by people known to me. And still, there were lots of others in the surrounding area. I was led to a stage of Light with multi-colored confetti falling from the sky.

Big celebration!

It was as if all the forms there in spirit were sparklers shooting off sparkles of gold and silver and the purest colors ever seen. A concert of Light.

I did immediately have thoughts of those left behind. What about my children? What about my children? What about my children and my family and the few people I really trusted?

How could I just leave like that? Just fade away!

My passing from the view of physical consciousness must have been like walking out of the spotlight of the stage into the shadows—and from there—into nothingness. At the same time, I was poised to recreate and expand (there in the physical world) past successes and establish an even more solid and rightful position as a dedicated and pure performer. That's something I needed in my head. Something I needed in my heart. Something I longed for in my Soul.

Those thoughts of my children and others were calmed almost as quickly as they crossed my consciousness. It would all be okay. In the end, it would all be okay. This is a universe of justice and peace. For once in my remembered existence, I didn't have to be guarded or afraid or closed or uncertain.

Before me on the stage, a swirling globe emerged from above. Literally, it was a swirling image of the World. Spinning. Descending. And it all connected to me.

A cord—from the Earth—connected to what would have been my heart when in physical form. A warm wash of energy surrounded and enveloped me.

I came to instantly understand that feeling to be the true essence of Love.

That's **Love** with a capital **L**.

What did I do then?

I did what came naturally to me. I found that it was very much like giving a concert on the physical plane. I was swaying, dancing, singing to the harmonic light wave energy that engulfed the state of perfected creativity of my inner being and captured the audience. I was doing moves that may have been mind-altering to some but they were automatic transcendence to me. Transcending dance.

When the concert came to an end, we all stood and applauded but the applause wasn't just for me. It was for all of us. Everyone there. Everyone connected to everyone there. Applause for being who and what we are. A knowing that it took all of us together for the experience to work.

From there, I was led backstage to a quiet, empty room. The only furniture in the room was an easy chair and a bed. I felt I had the choice of using the chair or the bed to rest, relax and unwind. And then, I was left alone in a darkness that wasn't really dark. It was a subtle, warm, cozy space, something like a room warmed by a fireplace. I chose the bed.

It wasn't until I lay down on the bed that I saw the mirror on the ceiling. A sudden wave of release and humor ran through me as I was indeed looking at the man in the mirror.

Have you ever felt a jolt of adrenaline rush through your body? What happened to me next was that kind of experience—in reverse. With what felt like waves upon waves of relief flooding through my being, I could literally **feel** each individual wave and release of pressure if I turned my attention to it.

Suddenly a lifetime of physical tension, fear and unrest just seemed to drain away—out of my being—transmuting itself into lines and waves and streams of dull-colored light. I watched as that dull-colored light danced and swirled its way around the room. And it then just disappeared.

For me, it was a total physical and mental recognition of tension and overly alert energy transforming into a calm, clear, flowing peace.

I'm not sure how much time was spent in that state of total relaxation. Time didn't really have any quality to it.

When I felt totally "filled up" and overflowing with peace, I noticed there was another presence in the room. This being had a quiet authority feel to it, but not the kind of authority and power that you understand or abuse on the physical plane. This was a personality with a depth of understanding, *knowing,* experience and wisdom.

This being looked at me and I mentally heard (but did not physically hear) the words, "And peace be with you." The feeling was similar to the feeling/knowing/understanding you have when you say "Amen" at the end of a prayer. A completion of sorts.

This being and I spent time going over the lifetime I had just left. It was quite fascinating. I **knew** I was talented but didn't fully recognize the scope of that when in the physical dimension because I kept the attention then on the continuance of creating, recreating and expanding the creation. I didn't feel a sense of power or domination as I relived the experience. Instead, I got the feeling of accomplishment, success—like the completion of an unwritten inner contract.

We watched/felt/saw the experiences one after another. And no. The visions weren't all major or what one would consider important life scenes.

There were little, quick flashes of small kindnesses I had experienced and those I shared with others.

There were flashes of stopping to look at the moon in the night sky, along with the spark of creation that could turn that small vision into a best-selling song—which is exactly what happened as the inspiration for *Thriller.*

Just think of it. That one gaze at the moon created a whole vision of a song and video that, in turn, captured the attention of so many. Energy that was everlasting. With a life of its own. Into infinity.

I was looking at rows and rows of notes—the written kind, not the musical kind—although they were energetically the same thing. Each note was just a phrase or a thought or an inspiration caught on a small piece of paper. Each had their own life, if attention was turned to it. Each had the possibility of being a number-one hit or album or invention or unlimited possibilities.

The potential from any one of those small sparks of inspiration could lead into a kind of greatness that is inconceivable.

I knew that the concert just performed was, in a way, the extension of life and Love that I was preparing for on Earth but got to complete here in Heaven. I know that I can create that same experience at any moment. In any time. In any space.

Inspiration. Creativity. Trust in yourself to follow through on a vision. That's what life is about.

Whether it's life on this side or the physical side, it all flows from Love. The base point—the origin—of all creation is Love.

Life. Love. Inspiration. Creativity. To be continued. . . .

--Michael

Carla
October 22, 2009

Is there anything you'd like to add, Michael?

Michael: Yes. Judgment. Judgment and choices.

I was more of an extension of flowing, physical Love energy than most humans could understand, absorb or relate to in the physical realm. It's the energy that brought me the most joy but it brought emotional pain into my life as well.

The power of Love is what the world will come to know if it's allowed. Just allowed. It is available for all to choose.

Judgment is a harsh monster that inflicts a brutal, deep scar on a soul. You are probably thinking right now that I'm talking about the judgment of others. That would be a normal assumption from the human point of view.

I am, however, talking about one's judgment against their own, individual, sacred being.

The past experiences of my life, as they relate to both my career and personal life, are very well known. As a human, I held both myself and others responsible for the emotional pain and suffering I incurred. From an illuminated perspective, I can see how I was more unkind to myself than anyone else could have been.

Self-judgment is the harshest emotional punishment a Soul can feel. When you judge yourself unworthy in any way—be it because of race, color, age, or whatever circumstance— you are literally placing a scar on your Soul that only you can heal.

Others have the right to make choices because of actions they perceive to be true or right or just. But if you allow the judgment from others to have a negative emotional effect on how valuable you are as a human being—in your heart and mind—it's like slicing through your innermost being with a knife.

I don't want this to be misunderstood.

It does not mean there are no rules of decency to be followed as far as others are concerned. I'm talking about dealing with your self—your emotions—your energetic being. I can't express this enough.

Be careful how you think of yourself. Always choose a higher thought. A more forgiving thought when you make a mistake. A more educated conscious choice when given the opportunity—which is almost every moment you breathe. Choose a kinder and more generous vision of your **self**. In other words, have **true** value in yourself rather than follow a path of egotistical thinking. Allow others to have their beliefs, too, but don't let that drive your life force.

Continue to believe in your **self** as a master of your own fate and allow faith in all that is good and true and right and fair to be your guide. I think you will find that if you allow that for your SELF, that others will allow it for you, too.

My soul had made a choice to deal with the emotional pain through music, lyric and dance. Those talents were, in effect, my savior. That choice was the major driving force of my life and my soul.

Do you think each choice makes no difference?

Remember when I related the crossing over and being brought into a quiet room with a bed and a chair? I chose to lie down on the bed. It was a choice that I didn't have to think about. I just did what felt right to me.

Little did I know that even that small choice was a choice of faith. I had already crossed into the environment of pure faith—Heaven, as you call it. Although I had indeed made a choice to do something as simple as choose to lie on the bed rather than sit in the chair, I didn't understand that by doing what felt right at the time and choosing the bed, I had left the chair open for my healing companion who would join me later. It was **his** seat, not mine.

Simple choices. Self-judgment. These things are worthy of some thought.

My energy will be staying with you as you finish this book. It's a choice of Love that I made a long time ago. Much longer ago than you can perceive right now.

You know there are loose strings—a phrase you will undoubtedly hear again while you are on this book journey. So, shall we go back to the discussion of the Moonwalk?

If you could measure—and you can—the amount of ingredients added to that spark that brings a life into the world, you would see that the yardstick of rhythmic talent I came with added up to about two and a half feet. The other half foot of my yardstick of ingredients was filled with an unreasonable amount of childlike thinking.

I was moonwalking long before it was ever shown on stage.

The movements, abilities and visions were actually in my mind even before I could walk.

There was a naïve part of me that truly believed I could back up—walk backward—and erase time. I could erase memories by walking backward—moonwalking away from them—rather than moving forward.

By the time this action was shown on stage, I had lived the vision in my mind for many, many years. So it wasn't something new and unique as far as my mind-body interaction was concerned. It was something I'd done for as long as I could remember. It was an escape for me.

I do believe this answer is more than you expected. Am I right?

To totally allow your **self** to be absorbed by sheer rhythmic movement is something few would allow themselves to feel.

To me, entertaining by allowing myself to be completely immersed in the creative moment was a visual example of faith, love and self-approval.

Allow it for yourself.

--Michael

Pamela
October 29, 2009

The following transmission from Michael came after having a hilarious experience of breaking into one of his songs and rhythmically acting it out one night on the streets of Manhattan. Later, when I wrote down the experience (detailed in more depth in my Epilogue), this transmission from Michael came flowing through.

Michael: We don't play with rhythm enough in our ordinary lives. That is why those who do and can—say, the great entertainers of the world, and right now I think of Sammy Davis Jr.—he was a MASTER of rhythm—that is why those who can play with rhythm become ICONS because they act out—they dream out—the dreams others have denied themselves. And that is why these icons, these entertainers, take on an importance far greater than they should—because it is a substitution for the gray, flat, rhythmless lives that most live. Factory lives, where the rhythm is that of MACHINES. Corporate lives, where demands and pressures make one lose all individual rhythm. Each person has a rhythm, even a melody, symphonies of melodies, unto themselves. Anything in life that dampens that rhythm—think armies!—is death to the spirit.

If there is anything I can leave with you, it's this: dance to your own tune. Dance to your own rhythm. And you will find that it will become a great choreography where nobody steps on each other's toes. Nobody kills another because their rhythm did not match.

The vision I leave you with: I see a great dance number that includes every soul, every body on the planet. Even those of you who think you can't dance, who think you don't have rhythm, you do! And as we come together, we hear the beginning beats, we start in a magnificent choreography, all together in the beginning, and then we break out. We watch each other do solos, then couples, then groups combine, inventing new steps, integrating old ones into new forms, spontaneous groups who have never met combine and create a step never heard or seen before, everyone applauds and laughs and then the little kids come up, with their newfangled steps and we all laugh and have cake and throw each other up in the air and we start again. We learn from each other in joy. We learn from each other in the rhythm of life. We learn from each other, our ear to each other's hearts.

Yes, we can do this. Imagine, we wouldn't even have TIME to start a war. We'd be dancing our heads off!

--MJ

"This is it. . ."

ABRAHAM LINCOLN

16th President of the United States

Born: February 12, 1809

Died: April 15, 1865

First Transmission: September 29, 2009

Pamela

Isn't it funny how something as routine as a ride home on the subway can suddenly be taken over by an alternate reality? There I was, just riding along, when my mind went to Abraham Lincoln and the words started tumbling out. I had to punch out notes on my phone! By the time I arrived home an hour or so later, I was ready to receive Abe's full transmission.

I hadn't thought much about the life of Abraham Lincoln since grammar school, but this historical icon surprised me by the quality of psychological darkness he held in his being. It was shocking to hear how he felt "at fault"—or rather, fully responsible for his own assassination. Even more stunning was his psychological explanation for the reason why, revealing a darker and more complicated side of himself not fully recorded by history. His intimate report of his after-life experience also gave us a glimpse as to how heaven helps to balance the extremes of the personality and support the multidimensionality of the soul.

Lincoln could also be funny (albeit unintentionally!). He mentions intimate moments with his wife and refers to a soup she regularly made for him, with surprising effect!

Most moving, however, were Lincoln's words about leadership, giving us solid reason why we should pray for all our leaders, even when we don't like them.

Pamela
September 29, 2009

What kind of insights did you glean from your life?

Abe: I had a karmic pattern with John Wilkes Booth, caught in a struggle over many lifetimes that we were playing out. Sometimes I was the persecutor, sometimes he—an animosity that had built up and a sense that both of us could not continue to exist in the same plane at the same time. The sense of heroism that has become attached to the image of Lincoln did not reflect my inner experience, which was tormented, full of anxiety and self-doubt.

Yet, in the midst of all that, an inner voice, a strong inner voice would rise up with great power and confidence and direct me to do things which others would look on as heroic in the face of opposition. This voice had a sense of right and wrong on the universal plane. But in my own inner experience, this stance was in direct conflict with the anxiety I felt about going through with it. You could see this torment in my face, in my eyes, in the exhaustion which overcame me, which was truly emotional exhaustion born of this conflict.

The night of the assassination, as I was getting ready to go to the theater, a black whirlwind, a black inner vortex, overtook me, one I could not ignore. There was a sense of destiny that night. As I was putting on my white gloves I felt somehow it would be the last time I would do this.

I watched the caisson roll by with my body and I felt sadder for the country than I did for my own self, or for my body, for which I had little attachment. It felt freeing to be out of the body; somehow that body was tied up with a lot of anxiety and fear and exhaustion. But I had grave misgivings for the country, how they would continue, who would take up the banner. Ulysses S. Grant did an admirable job but the country went in a new way. It was not for me to do it, like it was not for Moses to see the Promised Land. Or FDR to see the end of World War II, as I later viewed.

We who are the spirits of former leaders do stand by great presidents, truly, all leaders, who are open to receiving guidance. It is best that the countrymen themselves continue to pray for their leaders, even if they do not like them. Those prayers are reflected here and attract many souls to direct light. We who understand that level of leadership also try to be of comfort and guidance. But it all depends on the nature of the leader and his capacity to hear. In many instances in America this has not always been the case.

I became more spiritually awake after death as I was able to view the anxieties and torments from another perspective. Indeed, the continual karmic pattern with Booth reflected these inner torments in me and continued to attract them. As with many leaders, in my case, I was sent to a so-called lower realm to endure experiences and "jobs" to better understand those we served, to relearn humility. I did sink to a level in which there were tormented killers to better understand those intent on disruption and death. Once there, I saw these tendencies in myself, which had been repressed in my system and had been the ultimate cause of my depression. As a result, what occurred in my life—the brutal assassination—was a playing out of my inner repressions. All this I did learn, not from psychological teaching, but from experiencing the so-called shadow on another realm. There is a sound, loving bite to all this.

It seems to me there is a kind of checks and balances that goes on here, in the cosmic universe, a little like modern government—when it works right! I believe it is called the shadow side in colloquial psychology now. This is how kings become servants, and servants, kings; murderers become saints and lovers and vice versa. When seen from this perspective, one comes to understand the true equality of human beings. We are each acting out an aspect, a role, of which the other side also exists in us. As such, we are all alike, no matter the outer circumstances. Truly this is the rational platform for the highest spiritual truth. This is why we are all the same. Why we are all equal—in God's name.

God speed.
--Abraham Lincoln

Carla

For me, the connection with Abraham Lincoln also came tumbling in. So smooth, precise and easy. I could feel a deep sense of accomplishment and peace within his vibrational quality. It was so clear and matter-of-fact that it seemed as if he were tired of telling—or hearing—his own story. I doubt, though, that he's been specifically asked very many times about his crossing over.

The visions that came with the crossing were the most powerful I'd ever felt/seen/heard to date. It felt like I was literally riding on his long coattails with the same sensations one would feel on a roller coaster.

I could actually see the lines and rows and multitudes of soldiers—all in uniform, all saluting—and feel the respect each had for the other as we soared by. They all seemed to have an ingrained understanding for the grace of destiny.

At the time of "landing," I could feel a huge sense of relief for the long-earned, embraced by his Soul, time alone. It was like a quiet opening of a dam allowing the force of water to flow at its own will. Time held by Nature. A tree. A creek. No pressures or responsibilities.

When the moving clips of past remembrances had passed by on the water, an abundance of accomplishment and triumph took over. He was now ready to meet with those who had departed before—the first being his son Willie. That's the energy he wanted to reconnect with first.

Carla
September 30, 2009

Tell me about crossing over. The feelings. The sights. The sounds. . .all of it.

Abe: Extraordinary, this opportunity. My best to you and your companion in this venture.

So your interests at this moment lie in my crossing over. Exhilarating feeling. Yes, indeed.

I can feel your need for a visual example, so if you will, picture a man standing in the center of a doorway. His arms are stretched out, hands sturdy on the frame, as if to bolster himself from any movement. I was hesitant to go, rather similar to being in shock, I suppose.

There was an immediate questioning, on my part, as to whether this was another dream or if it were truly happening. I just let go, felt my body relax and was surrounded by a red, swirling sensation. Somewhat like being absorbed and melting into a red dust cloud.

At this point, although I had an interest in the color and its feeling (as though my mind was arguing with itself as to whether color had a physical feel to it), there proceeded to be people flying by me—or I was flying by them. It's hard to decipher.

There were so many. Lines and lines and lines of people. I guess you could equate it to a parade. People lined up for what felt like a long distance. Rows and rows of people.

There was no tunnel. It was as though I could feel the changing hues or sensations of colors as I passed through.

And the people. So many—uncountable—people.

Suddenly, the colors cleared to the brightest and most unclouded visual gift I had ever experienced. Miles and miles of waving wheat fields, which included a creek lined by huge sycamore trees.

I had the sense or knowing that I would be talking to or interacting with each person I had just passed. But, for the moment, I had the inspiration and desire to just sit for a while.

Alone. Under a big sycamore tree. Beside the creek.

I watched the water flowing by. Occasionally I had the thought that it was a creek of tears. But there was no negative emotional attachment to that thought. The water would flow, and then, on the spur of the moment, a short memory clip or picture reenactment of a past memory or experience would float along—much like watching a fallen leaf going down a lazy river.

I had the physical feeling of complete order and accomplishment. Completion in a way.

I can't express the sensation because there are no true words that encompass the feeling. It was not a feeling of victory, in that there was no pride or ego attached.

Completion.

It was much the same feeling I had when I finished splitting a large stack of wood. A remembrance of the physical delight of a body worn out and much exerted from honest hard work passed through my thoughts.

Order. Accomplishment. Completion.

Though many come to this side to find themselves greeted by family, friends and others passed before them, I had the exquisite honor of a more personal, one might say, "Reassembling of the Soul" time.

With the exception of traveling along the lines and rows of people, my "landing" was solitary, gentle and peaceful. I got the treasure of time and silence—the ability to piece myself back together—in PEACE.

How Soul inspiring!

When I was ready, there appeared a gentleman in a white robe, which was adorned with golden braids. He just suddenly appeared, sitting beside me. There was an inexhaustible depth of calmness, focus and comfort incorporated in his being that sprang forth and I seemed to devour its offering.

Through him, I instantly felt a total regard, understanding and respect for human life. I understood the years of tears flowing without the sad emotion, as I had felt while watching the creek earlier. It all came together. It all made sense. There was an ordered purpose for all that had come before.

Without saying anything out loud, he asked if I was now ready to meet with those who had been waiting for me.

My son! My son Willie.

What a joyful reunion that was! There were family and friends—so many. As I looked beyond those immediate spirits I could see soldiers, regiments of soldiers, all with smiles on their faces and respect in their eyes. Unimagined and unspeakable relief flooded through my being.

Order. Accomplishment. Completion.

I went through the lines and rows of people without tire. I seemed to absorb the contentment, inner-knowing and respect that passed between each of us. I knew them all.

There was some delay in time and space, but after settling into my new position and environment, after the greetings of all present, I turned around to view a sight that was humbling, to say the least.

Visually, in the physical, you would have seen me standing with my hands grasped together behind my body. I watched as the funeral train snaked its way toward its final destination. I watched as church bells rang their songs of sorrow. I watched as swarms of people, both friends and foes, stood silenced in the vision before them.

I watched on a personal level what God must watch as we go about our daily business.

I leave you with these thoughts. There is order. There is accomplishment. There is completion.

With utmost respect,

--Abraham Lincoln

* * *

Pamela
September 30, 2009

Is there anything more you would like to add?

Abe: From this standpoint we can look out on history and see the cavalcade of presidents and kings and queens, seemingly where the power is. There is a family line to these forms of leadership so in a sense there is a destiny to them. No matter how much you try, you cannot sway that pattern, that destiny to lead or be elected or to fall into the family that gives birth to leaders. But you can definitely screw it up and so have many dynasties. The spiritual DNA to lead, so to speak, does not always have embedded within it the gene— the pattern—for success. In fact you could be delivered into a family, a lineage of leaders that was, in essence, a screw-up, mountebanks.

But then again, one can cultivate leadership traits in oneself, and through this, in subsequent lifetimes, or even opportunities [*in life*] one can rise to the occasion, but even that has been set in some kind of destiny. The rush to take up the sword, the gavel, to lead people—what is it that gives one the confidence that one's opinions are worth pursuing? I struggled with this. I was at heart an intellectual who needed public opinion to boost my ego. But alas, my life story was to transcend that and indeed become a mediator between conflicting opinions.

Frivolous thoughts got in the way, as they do with most people. I am/was quite hard on myself. I grew up with a mother who was quite a taskmaster; there was a disciplinarianism in the family that made me uncomfortable with physical attentiveness and affection. My wife Mary found me cold, but I struggled inwardly about it. She often made me hot soup and I found this extraordinarily comforting. A sense of maternalism, soft and inviting, accompanied the gesture. It became a prelude to many moments of deep intimacy because something deep within me needed to be soothed.

Just the thought of this soup is very warming to the soul—and the body.

If I had to do things over, I would have sought more counsel during my presidency. And indeed, even before. Have more group advisory sessions. I often felt alone in the manner in which I was forced to make decisions, but luckily there was some inner guiding principle in me that assisted at the various critical junctures. I often had to support people in whom I felt ambivalent confidence due to the political nature of things. I would have surrounded myself with more higher souls in the Cabinet at that time. There was some religious fundamentalism that became obstacles to the forward movement of democratic ideals, as it seems to be repeated so throughout history. It is interesting to me how each leader in his day dealt with such extremists. It is the mark of a successful leader who knows how to deal with opposition in canny ways that bring people together, rather than cause more dissension.

If I were to do it over again? Each era will have its own challenge and definition of victory. We are coming to the close of an age in which the old ideals no longer serve. There must be a growing consciousness that is beyond individual countries or borders in order to bring about a group consciousness that is supportive of the very earth we live on. Peace at all costs can give rise to a fundamentalism that strikes terror at the heart of true peace-seeking men and women. Would that we would have leaders that see beyond the transparent violent nature of men and tap the very soul longings of all. It takes a man (or woman) in touch with his own soul to bring about this victory. A rare commodity, but more and more are moving into the position where that is possible. That is the work we do over here, to prepare and propel those ready to take this stand.

It is our only hope.

All in all, we must stop fighting brother against brother. And in the current time, a new definition of this "brother" must be gained. Likewise, it is seen that no country can stand alone against all the earthly and ecological challenges affecting the planet. Crisis will cause those to gather together who in the past have been brutal enemies. While we do not support the disintegration of the physical earth plane, we do view the coming challenges as a divine manifestation, as a divine impulse for those together to gather in One Name. This shall be done, with the help of great souls leading the masses.

It shall be done because that is the Great Plan that we are learning of.

--Abraham Lincoln

"We …who are open to receiving guidance..."

ALBERT EINSTEIN

Theoretical Physicist

Born: March 4, 1879

Died: April 18, 1955

First Transmission: September 27, 2009

Pamela

I was afraid to come close to Albert Einstein for many days. Maybe it was because I felt he was way too smart for me (the "how could I ever talk to a genius?" program acting up in my psyche).

But it's not like I hadn't talked to him before! Once, several years ago in a creative writing class, we had been asked to tackle an assignment that started with "I am..." and we were to fill in the blank and write. Somehow the name Albert Einstein popped into my awareness and I was off and running. The results even then were quite startling to me and my classmates—somehow I had touched a voice of far-reaching magnitude that deeply regretted not having loved more. Interesting, a similar theme returned this time, but from a broader viewpoint and with a much more insistent message. When I finally sat down for these transmissions from Albert, it was like he had always been sitting on my shoulder. I was surprised, and yet not surprised where his thoughts went—to the necessity for maternal love in the world as an active force of leadership. There is a very sweet, soft quality about him—he's not at all an inaccessible genius.

Pamela
October 20, 2009

Dear Albert Einstein, I am happy to make the acquaintance of yourself and your soul. In the spirit of our book, is there anything you would like to transmit through me according to the nature of your learnings on earth and the experiences you are having in the after-realm.

Albert: First, let me say I am very grateful to be a part of this project. It has repercussions that you do not know yet. If you could see the interconnections between people and ideas, between thought realms—yes, there are things such as that—then you would in essence become a thought traveler, a time traveler through thought. All thought would be accessible to you.

In my brief stay on earth—it feels brief within the eternity in which we are steeped—the ocean of eternity—I was able to swim or dive into that ocean without exactly knowing how I did it. I was able to access part of these realms with an assurance and ease that I could not be credited for. It was a given, although I did not always understand nor did I wish to. In fact I had a bit of superstition that kept me from thinking more deeply about how and why it could occur—this brain of mine, so to speak, this ability to transverse cause and effect. I had a private language that took me there, something in the flavor of a code that is not worth sharing because it had only relation and meaning to me, but once I recited that code internally—I believe it must have worked once—then I used it again and again. Perhaps it was superstition, perhaps it was inner training, Pavlovian, so to speak, that triggered that waiting part of my brain to access realms far beyond normal human comprehension. It did feel like flying through realms of thought passing by my awareness. I could stop it at any time and look further into it.

Often I was perceived by others as being lost in space, lost in time. Indeed I was in a greater time and space but not so clearly lost [ha ha]. I was being found by these ideas as I was finding them. There was a great love about it that is hard to explain. These thoughts and I loved each other. Does that sound insane? I think perhaps because we were discovering each other, like lovers, inhabiting the same time and space in our own little cocoon. One could become fascinated with the process. I was. And it was sometimes— most often—to the detriment of human relationships.

I was a seeker of wisdom, a thought traveler, so to speak. I was mesmerized by logic and what lay beyond logic. These are realms; these are very much realms that one can inhabit and beings do. Would one live their whole existence there?

At a certain point, a need to balance comes about and one learns from these realms what is indeed not there—the core of the feeling heart, the compassionate heart, sacrifice, givingness, surrender. One cannot really surrender to a number and so the ecstasy of the interplay is different. Definitely, the human heart wins over.

It is the very challenge of the present human on this planet to learn how to balance head and heart. So much can be advanced for the sake of humanity but it has to be balanced. So much knowledge can be had—it is there for the taking—it is right there to be plucked like apples off a tree—you can know anything!! Anything!!! But if it is not balanced by the human heart, by all the qualities we associate with the loving mother's heart, then it is no good and is in fact worse than no good. It is bad, it is destructive, it is nihilistic.

If you look at any dictator throughout history, there was always a problem with the mother's heart in relation to the son. I will stake my life on that.

So here is Albert Einstein saying what I believe to be the greatest world truth I can give: take care of the mothers. Teach. Nourish. Keep them safe. Honor them. Nourish them to become the holders of this light and they will give birth to children who will be commendable and bright and know how to take knowledge from the tree and infuse it with light and love.

I know this does not sound like Albert Einstein who spoke in odd mathematical symbols, but I would like to say E=MC squared—really means Energy equals Mother Care squared.

That's it. Please believe this and take it to heart. It is for the rescue of this world.

--Albert Einstein

Carla

Although I've had times of connection with Einstein's essence in the past, this is the first I've requested information on his experience of crossing over.

He seems to have quite a sense of humor and his essence is very light and personable.

I continually asked him to slow down his thoughts so that I could keep the interaction in some kind of order. His consciousness was moving so swiftly and he seemed to have so much to talk about. He was actually relaying information about two things at the same time—somewhat like "downloading" two thought packets simultaneously. One packet was the crossing-over experience. The other packet was his excitement about how things work—universally. He was fast-thinking...on the GO!

Carla
October 7, 2009

Tell me about crossing over. The feelings. The sights. The sounds...all of it.

Albert: My journey back was like an ignited rocket zooming off into space. Racing past the stars and moons and galaxies to a place where I'd been more connected to, over my lifetime, than I had been with the earth plane. If I looked closely at any bright particle, I could see equations and formulas—the kind that made me long to stop and evaluate—but the velocity of my movement kept me on the straight and narrow.

No people. I didn't pass any people nor were there spirits present on my "landing," as you call it. At some point, I realized that there were no souls present because I didn't have a truly emotional connection with people while on the earth plane.

Oh, they weren't far away. I could feel them, see their sparkles and reunite with them at any time I wished. My energy system was already moving at their approximate velocity, so there was no hurry to reconnect.

So the passing was fast (but remember, time is an illusion) and the landing was right on target, as I knew it would be. It was well calculated, so to speak [chuckling].

Back to the people.

Much of your emotional attachment quota is built within your DNA. Most will not understand this. Nor will they care. But as we come into the physical life, we are already programmed, in both our physical and spiritual DNA, with certain energetic components for our life.

Let's look at this as if we were a chef putting things together to make one sensational recipe. You might say that I had 3/4 cup of mathematical foundation and only room for 1/10 cup of emotional relationship space. We are all put together in this fashion, and as a chef I added a large amount of mathematics to my internal recipe.

Since Michael Jackson is an integral part of your book recipe, let's turn to an example of him. You may look at him through this ingredient lens and see that he had 3/4 cup of entertainment talent and the remaining 1/4 cup of his spirit was in search of pure love and acceptance.

Is this making sense to you?

DNA is rather like degrees of light. You may be born with a DNA storage that demands you have blonde hair rather than dark hair. It's the same with the natural rhythm of each unique individual. Some have a blueprint that is fulfilled with math and science. Others will be filled with music or dance.

There is a larger measurement of consciousness that remains hooked or anchored to this side (Heaven). The electronic waves or strings travel back and forth on that connection. I don't believe I ever really fully left this side (nor does anyone), but I seemed to leave more of my connection to this side than others prefer to do. That is why my trip "back" was so quick and easy. I had very little physical consciousness to release during the process.

There is so much to talk about as far as consciousness is concerned. Some are charted as genius. Others are not so. A mistake is made, however, to deem one better than or more important than the other. All are important ingredients in the collective vision and Divine Plan of life.

But you didn't ask me about all that. Did you? So I return to my journey toward Home.

Most humans don't choose the rapid ascent that I made. As you cross from physical life back to your spirit and soul's side of life, you release not only the physical remnants (your body) but also emotional and mental (non-physical yet weighty) elements. In tight physical form, these elements all work together to literally hold a person together.

There are virtually uncountable bits of conscious information held within your mind and body at any particular time. On the return to the spirit side of life, one basically releases the physical world from the inside out. First the body, and then the invisible fields of consciousness connected to the body.

There is what some would call a particle density barrier between the physical and spirit plane of life. Let's say it's a sifter of sorts. Dense, physically related particles will not pass through that sifting station and fall back to (or continue to stay in) the physical plane of life. There is a parameter, which is measured by velocity and clarity, to all elements in the spiritual plane. In other words, negative thoughts, emotions, experiences, physical form, etc., will not survive on this side due to their density. Those elements drop off as you transfer from the physical life to spirit life.

Once landing, I enjoyed watching as numbers and equations literally danced in front of me. What a symphony to my eyes that was. It was during that time that I was reconnecting with my true Soul by enjoying the movie or life review. I had little emotional value to release.

Within a short while, I moved toward the other dancing sparkles of Souls. It is a great reunion. For, from a heightened, pure, clear state of consciousness, we realize how unique and perfect we each are—just **as** we are.

One last thought about your connection to this side of life. From my point of view, one of the great things about life on the earth plane is the ability to take a nap. If you need to reconnect with your true spirit or to anything on this side, all you have to do is take a nap. We can explain more about this later if you wish.

--Albert Einstein

Carla
November 4, 2009

The last time we talked, I felt you had more to say but our connection was not focused at that moment. Can you continue now?

Albert: You see how little I care to discuss myself. I am no different than any man and there is no real reason to dwell on my emotional or physical connections while on the earth plane. My life was as my life was to be. We follow a divine plan.

I preferred the comfort of science above the comfort of humans. So we are again back to programming and envisioning the unseen.

Where do you want to go first?

DNA? Time? Space? Quantum physics? Tell me your pleasure and I will try to focus those thoughts to you and we will keep to the short version.

Consciousness. Consciousness is your first choice and a good choice that is.

I know that one of the things you have been pondering over the past years is the speed of thought. Thought travels much the same as light but with more velocity.

Thought is a shape-shifter of sorts in that it can be observed as a wave or a particle depending on the observer.

Light has the same method of measurement (waves or particles), but it is heavier than thought and therefore visible and more easily measured.

Until it is observed, thought (like light) exists in a state of animated suspension and only presents itself as a wave or particle according to the one who observes it.

If you look at life with this quantum-life vision, do you now see how even a very small thing will affect how you create your reality? Amazing, is it not?

So now, let's compare thought to consciousness. Do you understand that you start to bend over to pick something up before you have even dropped it? This is how prepared the physical realm is to live through reaction. You react before you act.

That reaction response is woven into physical reality's DNA. Once this is understood, you can very easily break almost any ingrained pattern.

When you start to raise your consciousness by becoming more aware or through a decision to operate with less reliance on programmed reaction, you are truly creating your reality in a much different way than through the patterned, automatic response as before.

Now do you see how the Law of Attraction, which has been so popular recently, works? By becoming aware of the "Law," one breaks a patterned response and opens up to more exaggerated or expanded possibilities.

And now, for the purposes of this book, we will move on to DNA. When you are part of the physical realm, you are also still anchored on this side—the spirit side of life.

One can draw inspiration from this side at any time. You only have to allow it. Whether that inspiration is music or art or science, it is always available and connected to you through your spiritual DNA.

Ninety-nine percent of all human DNA, as it is scientifically known presently, is the same. It is only that one percent difference that makes you unique. But that one percent makes you extremely unique in every way. There is more to your DNA than has been proven at this time, but the discovery is not far off.

The invisible, spiritual side of your DNA holds the experience and knowledge blueprint to any physical lifetime. And even more interesting is the fact that the spiritual DNA is changing and expanding all the time. Physical DNA is more contained and less expansive due to the fact that it **is** physical. It therefore holds the same pattern at all times because of the substance density required to be tangible.

In times like the present, with the expanded ability for scientific measurement, I occasionally wish for a further allotment of time and space on the physical side of life. The possibilities are so very exciting and precise.

So how and why does that spiritual DNA change and expand? By developing awareness. By expanding consciousness. Through conscious choices. By recognizing experience, knowledge and wisdom. By dissolving the need to unconsciously react to repeating patterns of action.

For each instance of **conscious** choice that allows something better for yourself and others as a human being, you expand the collective consciousness and break a pattern of unconscious repetition. Every conscious thought counts!

Some would call that love. Others would say it's the Golden Rule. I would say it is life as it was meant to be lived with respect for yourself and others.

There are many ways to create a new meaning for scientific equations already in existence. Just use your imagination. Imagination is more important than knowledge.

For those on this side (and yours), we will close this conversation with the very familiar equation of $E=MC^2$.

Energy. The basic component of energy is nothing more or less than consciousness. It is the concentration of light and thought at speeds yet uncalculated.

Energy equals Mass Consciousness squared.

So what is mass consciousness squared?

Your perception, plus the awareness of all those on the physical plane at this time, hold the brilliant pattern of physical life. In other words, you and all things physical are the guardians of all things physical. You are the "M"—the Mass--in the equation.

The "physical" mass consciousness measurement is then multiplied by the collective wisdom or consciousness on this spirit side of life. In other words, your collective knowledge times the collective knowledge on this side of life. Those of us on the spirit side of life are the "C" in the equation.

This combination is then squared by the initial source of all that is. God. The Universe. Insert the word of your choice.

There is no way to explain in words how important each life is and there is no way to separate your life from others— whether in the physical or spiritual realm—for they are one and the same.

It is the ultimate equation.

Light speed and more. . .

--Albert Einstein

"I was in a greater time and space . . ."

AMELIA EARHART

Aerial Pioneer

Born: July 24, 1897

Missing: July 2, 1937

First Transmission: September 27, 2009

Pamela

I approached Amelia with some trepidation. I had no idea how to contact her (that feeling of unknowing always makes me nervous), but when I started repeatedly to see advertisements on TV for a new film about her, I felt she might very well be our next subject. One day I felt the impulse to find a photo of her online and was immediately struck by her energetic resemblance to the actress Angelina Jolie (both loved flying); when I finally located their childhood photos and placed them next to each other, I nearly dropped my laptop—they looked like the same person! Other inspirations abounded. In the week between transmitting Albert Einstein and Amelia, I was in the midst of looking for writing jobs, and minutes before channeling Amelia, I boldly answered an ad at an agency which had ignored the year before, putting me in that "what the heck" kind of mood. With the bravado of someone who had nothing to lose, I signed my query letter with a tagline that popped out of nowhere: "Pamela Bloom—Thinks like a woman. Writes like a man. Creates like a genius." I thought it was just a joke, but a few minutes later, I had the urge that Amelia wanted to speak.

Pamela
October 18, 2009

Dear Amelia, do you have anything you would like to share with us for this project? In my case, what were the learnings you had on earth?

Amelia: Live like a man inside a woman. This was my motto, my internal slogan. Both aspects are fundamental to the entire experience of life, of living, of creative expression, of adventure. Live like a man inside a woman. This, I determined, was the best option, despite all the challenges, despite needing to look backwards whenever you looked forwards. It takes a certain kind of personality to do this but the rewards were great.

I never considered my final end a tragedy. I died in the heights of bliss, literally, doing what I was meant to do— flying as a free agent. It was actually good the body was not disturbed for some time as I was able to make a transition organically without much hoo-haw. Later people would mourn and I was able to watch from a distance, but I would not have wanted to be that close to the action of such grief. It would have dampened the spirit, so to speak, and brought me closer into a shaky landing.

The flight of the soul. The passion of the imagination to throw the mind into outer space. This courage, this fearlessness, perhaps, has been owned by men throughout the duration of history, but it is NOT a possession of the male gender—this is what my soul screamed to realize in this life. Nor is sensitivity simply the possession of women. In coming days, in this coming time of history, we will be able to see androgynous beings—women in men, men in women, who are not freaks, not beings to laugh at, but full-fledged human beings in spirit form, with a balance of all aspects weighing the scales at neutral.

There are in your present society many—a number—of pioneers who understand what I am saying. They are not flamboyant in the sense they have exaggerated features of either sex; they are slowly and surely coming to terms that every mood, every sensitivity, is available to each and every gender when you take off the limiting blinders we have given to gender.

The question is, why have we done this to ourselves— created these definitions that blind us to our true power, our true reality, our true ability to soar, soar, SOAR! We are as great as any eagle; we are the beings the Creator intended, and thus we have every aspect available to us. When I looked around in my life, I did not see restrictions, I did not see limitations. If there was unhappiness around me, it was simply because those around me could not keep up. That is the sacrifice one pays. Easy to fall into the traps, but trod I did out of them, eventually. When I found my power, when I found this "thing" inside me that said, "Amelia, soar," then there were no barriers, no restrictions, no fences of any kind holding me back.

This is the Man in Woman we must find. It is for a Man to dare to find the Woman inside that will set that path for others. Look for him/her perhaps in a great singer, in a great artist, in a great contemplative. You have many to choose from. Look further into them and see what they are indeed accomplishing along this same path.

This is the path of unity of all aspects of the Divine.

--Amelia Earhart

* * *

Carla

Amelia. She seemed to be showing up everywhere. I had the feeling when we started this project that she would be a part of it. It's interesting she was the only woman included in this book of men. That fit her personality (and message) so well.

What I didn't expect was her recount of crossing over.

Preconceived ideas! I was being reminded of how automatically we think. It would be a natural assumption to think her crossing would involve flight or flying sensations. But I was taken totally by surprise!

No flight. No flying.

Her account had me wondering about the last moments of her life and if there was, perhaps, some correlation with her demise and crossing. Maybe we will have an answer to that question in the near future. Maybe not.

All I know is that there was a sense of courage, honesty and proud achievement to her essence. No "hoopla," as she called it. Just the sense of a job well done.

Carla
October 14, 2009

Tell me about crossing over. The feeling. The sights. The sounds. . .all of it.

Amelia: You would think my passing would be related to flight or flying but it was actually quite quiet, quick and almost like slipping through an underwater cave. Although I wasn't too fond of water play when in my body, the passing gave me the feeling of being a mermaid. That's a lovely picture, isn't it?

It was body and water in fluid movement with each other—much like body, mind and air working together when flying. I often think that I passed out of that lifetime much the way I came in at birth. Body and water in fluid movement with each other.

I was greeted by a small group of friends and family on arrival, which is how I wanted it. No hoopla. I had an understanding that I could have a ticker tape parade if I wanted—at any moment I wished. It wasn't necessary.

Honestly, although I knew there was much more I could have accomplished in my lifetime, I was satisfied with the results I had achieved with the exception of my last flight. The incompletion of that journey was totally my responsibility.

My consciousness left my body before the flight's conclusion. It was like I was moving ahead in time before any of the physical actions came to pass.

Don't misunderstand me. It isn't that I was disappointed in not physically and consciously completing that flight. I was disappointed for all the people who passionately believed in and supported me. During the crossover time, I had a lingering feeling of disappointment in myself. I had let them down.

I now understand that all things happen exactly as they should.

Most of my lifetime was spent trying to feel the freedom of spirit that is the norm on this side. The thrill of flight often consumed me so much that all other sensations—sights, sounds, touch, tastes—were shut out in a vacuum of perpetual yet suspended speed.

After the reunion, I went to a small dark room alone to watch a review of the life I'd just left—very much like a movie theater. It was fun to watch but still left a slight melancholy feeling connected to my consciousness. Upon that thought, however, there was the instant running of another "movie" showing me the out-reaching effects of what I'd accomplished.

Something inside me knew I wouldn't return when I left on that flight. But there was no turning back. It was a flight of destiny. I had accomplished all I'd come to do in that lifetime and no one ever leaves the earth plane without fulfilling their plan.

Little girls no longer had to dream of being pilots. The door was now wide open. Although I knew my actions had opened a lot of doors for others in the future, I was touched while being shown a clip of a small girl sitting on her front lawn with her arm wrapped around her dog.

She was looking upward at the horizon—watching the exhaust stream of a jet. When this little girl's life flashed forward, I could see her as the pilot of a large jetliner, making a smooth landing—one of many she made each year taking passengers from one place to another. That image gave me more pleasure than all I'd accomplished for myself.

Have you ever felt overwhelming relief? It's that feeling of calm that rushes through your being, leaving an instant relaxation of body, mind and spirit. That's how I felt when I landed.

Relief. Success. Completion.

It's a feeling that can be the standard during one's lifetime. Isn't it time you allowed that feeling without waiting to arrive on this side for it to be so?

--Amelia Earhart

Carla
November 9, 2009

Amelia: I know I've been on your mind for the past few days. Making a connection may be a better way to put it. You had thoughts of incompletion as far as our communications were concerned.

When you have thoughts that don't "go away," there is indeed leftover energy that needs to be addressed. Please comprehend that I am talking about incomplete energy on any subject, not just our communications. It would be good for those on the physical plane to understand this detail, trust their intuition and pay attention to any "incomplete" feelings, no matter what the source.

The one word you've thought of as it connects to me is "courage." This is for more reasons than the personal attachment you have to my poem on courage.

I do have more to communicate on that subject, if you are ready.

I got extreme pleasure from words, their formation, meanings, changing them around, and how they blended together in works of literature during my lifetime. In all honesty, I would have been as happy being an author as I was as an aviator. Both actions were a big part of my soul's flame. Both were fun for me. Life is about having fun.

That courage poem came to me in a flash of inspiration as I was staring out a window one day, watching trees blowing in the wind. I wasn't thinking of courage at the time but the word grabbed me with some impact anyway. I always trusted anything that had the force of impact behind it.

When I said "courage is the price that life exacts for granting peace," it was a phrase that had bubbled up from my Soul from the very time I was a little girl.

It does, at times, take courage to act on your inspirations and dreams, although it shouldn't. It took a certain amount of courage for me—both mental and physical—to achieve my dreams of flight. Physical flight. Mental flight.

We are never given a thought, dream or goal without those thoughts, dreams or goals being within reach. We are also never given a problem, difficulty or challenge without there already being an attainable solution for same.

Really think about this for a moment. Let the full truth of those statements impact your mind. How would truly **knowing** these facts change your way of thinking about life?

The poem continued with "the Soul that knows it not knows no release from little things." The Soul understands the courage it takes to even think of agreeing to a physical lifetime. To leave this place of everlasting life, harmony, security and knowledge—for a physical lifetime born into a cultural belief of struggle and sacrifice—can be an overwhelming responsibility. Even if you know you will eventually return to grace.

If you look at the words—courage and responsibility—through an open lens, you will see that courage is simply the ability to respond. To any action. To any experience. To any challenge.

Courage comes from the strength of the soul. It's an ingrained blessing born into every living thing.

Courage—inborn courage—is an ability that is often overlooked and yet so easily called upon when necessary.

Courage allows a mental and emotional release of pressure by granting the ability to respond. To understand the grace of your soul, you must only consciously have the knowledge that timeless courage is available through the simple act of leaning upon it. And this includes both small and large responsibilities.

Courage is an energetic quality embedded in your essence. It's available for you to lean on whenever it is needed.

--Amelia Earhart

"The flight of the Soul . . ."

PAUL NEWMAN

Actor, Philanthropist, Race-Car Driver

Born: January 26, 1925

Died: September 26, 2008

First Transmission: October 18, 2009

Pamela

Paul Newman was a charmer. His eyes first called me to him—right through a photograph I saw one Sunday in the New York Post. For about a week he had been dashing in and out of my consciousness, and this one particular photo, taken by the writer Gore Vidal in the late 50s, seemed to seal the deal: the actor was lying entangled in the arms of friends, with his wife Joanna leaning over, and it felt as if the light in his famously beautiful eyes were streaming out to meet mine. Just as we were wondering who would be our next interviewee, a few words related to the idea of "focus" started to come through from Paul, but Carla told me to wait. Continuing to receive more, I e-mailed her a few days later and she said, "Go for it." Those three words of encouragement kicked off a torrent from Paul. His energy felt very virile and salty—yet joyous and engaged, and much deeper than I would have ever imagined. A full spirit. A profound soul. And still full of zest!

Pamela
October 18, 2009

Dear Paul Newman, Do you have anything you would like to share with Carla and me regarding the learnings you had on earth or your view of heaven?

Paul: Heaven is what you make of it. I love it! Imagine standing in a circle and turning slowly around and you receive this kaleidoscopic, Technicolor, ever-shifting vision of reality. Multilevel, multiplex [ha ha], multi-dimensional. Everything MULTI. Like a multidimensional chess set that blows your mind by the number of levels and patterns and movements. I spend a lot of time doing this very slowly, turning my awareness around slowly—just as if I were standing in one spot—and moving like a clock. I am in awe of the wonder, astonished by the multi-complexity of the divine creation, of the divine creator's mind.

We have no idea on earth.

Absolutely no friggin' idea!

This idea of focus often fascinated me on earth. That is why I was so drawn into car racing. The level of intense focus made sure that I was in the present moment. It was a life-or-death situation if you lost focus. Not only for yourself, but also your car, your teammates, the other drivers. It was like being in war. You may see one driver, but the truth is, you cannot drive successfully unless you develop intense one-pointed focus as well as a very grand, broader focus that includes the interdependency of all involved. I love this feeling. I loved the speed, the risk, but there was a soul feeling to it. A definite soul attraction. Now I understand this attraction by having this experience I am having [*the kaleidoscopic one*] in what you so-call Heaven.

It is simply the after-life of consciousness. Consciousness that continues and is eternal. The God-consciousness in us all.

You might ask, what did this focus have to do with the rest of my life? With acting? In truth, when an actor has this kind of focus on stage, he/she is magnetic. It draws the audience in. They resonate with this attention, this kind of one-pointed focus bathed in a bigger awareness field because they themselves crave to find this within themselves. I only understood this partially while in my life as Paul. I was compelled to it as one is compelled to the sweet smell of oranges or whatever your taste is. Fried onions, whatever. Popcorn! You are compelled organically to this state of mind because you are ultimately that state of mind.

But so many people walk around tired, unawake, sleeping, really. Most of the world is walking around with blinders.

If I can say anything of import, it is this state of mind which is one of the most important things to cultivate. There is a freshness in it, a relaxation and an energy at the same time. I was able in acting to access it at times. I often found myself staring off into space when I was working on roles and found myself gliding into that space. When I was immersed in that state, then I would go over lines, somehow allowing the emotion of the moment to be focused within that center point and yet retaining that relaxed open awareness—what I called earlier the "grand broadness."

Now looking from this perspective, I see that people responded to what seemed like a laid-back quality in my stage presence and yet a masculinity, a virility. All this was born from these states of mind I worked with. Some of it was done unconsciously. Some of it not. I had had acting training but I found my way through this instinctually.

I did have a feeling of gratitude for the good things in life. Of course there were challenges, my son's death. All this deepened me to care more about others, to realize my place in their lives, to see how I could make a difference. And I wanted to. It was great happiness that the charities and businesses that supported those charities were done in collaboration with my daughter. It felt my son was approving this, helping us. I rarely talked about this, but I did feel his presence. We have made amends here. He is one of the kaleidoscopic experiences I witness everyday.

What more can I add?

Forgive others. From this kaleidoscopic awareness, you cannot possibly imagine what you do not know of The Plot. The Great Plot we are all living out. You are only given your own lines, and few, if ANY, know the entire script. Respect other's lines, don't go walking all over them. Every one has a role. Don't get stuck in one. Reinvent yourself constantly. The curtain must come down sometime.

The theater is more than a metaphor.

It is life.

--Paul Newman

* * *

Carla

Paul Newman had such a young feeling to his essence. A kind of everlastingly youthful quality that felt so open, expanded and free. He was focused in his delivery but still had a light, whimsical feel. It reminded me of someone who was "in the moment" and enjoying every bit of it.

I could almost feel him wanting to break into some kind of comedic set that would bring laughter to everyone who came close. And yet, his focus seemed to harness that energy so it could be transferred in complete thoughts.

There was a point in his transmission where he talked about how a terrible emotional experience could be turned into something good and somehow rewarding. I hadn't known about the death of his son until Pamela told me later, but the image I got when he was relaying this message was of his son and the organization he had started in his son's honor. He didn't specifically bring up either his son's name or the name of the organization, but I know that's what he was referring to.

To me, it was like he was feeling and describing the big and small picture at the very same time while absolutely delighting in the energy. Very fun. Very light.

Wow! He still has a magnetic quality—in every sense of the word. I think he must have come into this lifetime with 3/4 cup of sexy.

Carla
October 21, 2009

Paul, tell me about your experience crossing over. The sights. The sounds. The feelings.

Paul: Wow. What a ride! It was like being able to see, hear and feel everything at once. Which is, I guess, exactly what it is to some extent.

If you could bundle up all the beautiful music you've ever heard, heighten the impact of all the colors you've ever seen and multiply all the good sensations you've ever felt—that's what it was like.

Whoa, Nelly. It was amazing.

I expected to go. It was time. So my transition was more like I already had one foot on the other side. All I had to do was pick up the foot still planted here and let go.

I understood that I had actually been working on this journey for two months before I passed over. So the trip itself was quick and yet full of impressions. You can literally **feel** the colors and sounds vibrating through you as you pass from one existence to another.

There was a swirl of emotion and understanding, which was also a part of the experience. The emotion is what drives you through a "life review" and it's laced with the complete understanding of the how and why of life events. It's so cool when you see the big picture—in Technicolor.

The landing on this side was like sitting through a marathon of my movies. The difference is, I was watching myself act out my life rather than a script. Had there been a script to follow? Oh, yes. There sure was. And now, it was totally understandable.

I spent some time watching this blue-eyed me reliving life and found a sense of peace holding my heart. The intense times of loss suddenly had a purpose when I could see no true purpose to them during my lifetime.

That's important to know. I mean, **really** understand. Everything does happen for a reason.

I felt ageless. Confident. Eternally cool. Not from an ego or cocky perspective but from a fulfilled life point-of-view.

After the life review, I went to a joyous reunion with friends, family and actors I'd worked with during my lifetime. It was like a banquet or celebrity roast. Lots of laughs. Lots of hand-shaking and congratulating each other.

To see my old friends and at the same time understand how our lives all fit together was just amazing. It made me yearn to sit down with them, have a cigar and talk over old times!

I had to laugh at myself and all those times during my life where I thought there was no good reason for an event to happen. I had plenty of faith in myself during my life but didn't have faith that things happened exactly as they should for all concerned. Boy, was I wrong.

Yes. Even the times that were devastating emotionally had good purpose. Because every action we take has an effect on others. And sometimes, we can take those emotional hits and turn them into life-affirming events for others. That's what counts.

Whether it's true life or a movie, we change our life and the lives of others with each breath we take, with each scene we act, with each lap we complete.

Life here, as with life on the earth plane, is what you make it. So my best advice is to always choose the most exciting and

unforgettable role. Make your life an Oscar-winning
performance. And have faith in yourself in each second.

--Paul Newman

"The theater is more than a metaphor. . ."

WALT DISNEY

Animator, Entertainer, Director, Entrepreneur

Born: December 5, 1901

Died: December 15, 1966

First Transmission: October 30, 2009

Carla

I felt Walt Disney's presence for about two weeks before he came through. And although he wasn't tapping his foot impatiently, he was definitely ready to talk.

Next thing I knew, all matter of coincidence (which I don't believe in—coincidence, that is) started happening. Almost every commercial that came on the TV was suddenly attached to Disney in some way. This happened five or six times until I heard, "Hi Ho, Hi Ho. It's off to work we go." I knew then that it was time to start taking notes.

My first impression was that this crossing was going to live up to the expectations I had beforehand. I also knew there was a lot of humor coming up with some hidden meaning behind it. For example, there is reference to a private joke between the great Walt Disney and myself.

You will read his mention of the "It's A Small World" ride. On a trip to Disneyworld, I was stuck on that ride when it broke down. For what seemed like hours, the Small World tune played over and over and over. That can almost be considered torture as far as I'm concerned.

Walt was warm and personable. There was a sense of wonder and magic to him still. At one point he mentioned his not being alive to see the completion of Disneyworld. After our connection, I looked up his life and sure enough, he didn't live to see the completion of that magical kingdom. It's small things like that—a line thrown out in the conversation or a fact not known beforehand—that makes these conversations so exciting and real to me.

When I teach Tarot, I tell my students that the less you know about a person, the better the reading. This is true because you have fewer ideas/judgments/thoughts of your own to "get in the way" through the reading. It's just as true in working on this book. Those little facts are what some would call proof. To me, it's just a sign that I'm on track and to continue on in the same way.

Carla
October 23, 2009

Tell me about crossing over. The feelings. The sights. The sounds. . .all of it.

Walt: This is the one you've been waiting for, huh? [laughing].

Yes. The crossing-over experience for me was like taking a wild ride at one of my magical kingdoms. There was the sense of a tunnel but it was an "open" tunnel with expanding sides and length. There wasn't a bright light at the end of the tunnel. Instead it looked like I was swirling toward a large fireworks display.

Trust me. It wasn't like taking the It's a Small World ride [laughing again].

Although I always lived with a somewhat larger vision of life or creativity made physical, I was still amazed at the vast and expanding trip I found myself on. Wow.

If you can picture me taking a fast roller-coaster ride through stars and galaxies, that's what it was like. It totally snowed under the miniature worlds I had created in my theme parks. As the thought of each creation passed through my consciousness, whether it be rides at Disneyland or the Snow White movie, I pictured each creation as if it were in a snow globe.

There was a teacup ride snow globe.

A Snow White snow globe.

A Cinderella snow globe.

I knew that if the glass were broken on any of the snow globes, the creation would be birthed and come into a life of its own.

I was moving quickly but knew I could stop at any time and swirl through any galaxy or snow globe to see other miniature "make-believe" worlds available there. And all of these worlds were just as real as anything created on earth.

So here I was, enjoying the journey. Totally fascinated by some of the sights. I did stop, or at least slow down, in a few places. It was as though I could see worlds and universes that I had a chance to create but didn't.

The colors and songs were enchanting as anything I've ever seen, and I've seen a lot of enchanting things, as you know. Each was so pure and dancing with **life**! Wow!

So it seemed as though I swirled through this magnificent energy for quite some time before coming to the "landing" point. I could have stayed suspended in that magic if I wanted, but I also knew there was an energetic substance to it that I could visit at any time I wished.

In some respects, I had the fleeting thought that I would be greeted by Mickey and Minnie Mouse at the landing. They were real enough to me to have been family.

I was, however, greeted with a parade in my honor. Yes. Just like the parades at Disneyworld. Fireworks. Happy, smiling people—lines and lines of them. And I got to ride on a float.

Now, you may not know it, but that vision, which was taking

place at Walt Disney World, was important to me because I didn't live to see the completion of that dream while in the human body.

When I reached a version of Cinderella's castle, some of my old friends and family were standing on the steps. All waiting to celebrate the life and worlds we had all worked to create.

And yes. I was met by a few Mickey's and Minnie's, among others. They were some of those wonderful souls who had acted a part at Disneyland—in costume—but had passed on before me.

I understood that so much credit was given to me when, in fact, I had not earned that credit. Since I had taken some of that recognition during my life, I had some instant regrets about that subject, for sure. I was not an easy man to get along with at times. That understanding did lay a little heavy on my consciousness both in life and now on the other side.

While on the earth plane, I could be a very harsh, almost ruthless—bordering on cruel—employer and friend. I knew I would be going through a time of life review because the emotions that swelled up inside me were leading me to the fact that I would be addressing this issue again.

But first, I had what could be seen as a parade and then a banquet to attend inside Cinderella's castle. Perhaps I would be meeting some of those inside that I needed to make amends with.

So the parade came to an end, and after the personal greeting, we all moved inside to a magical scene of magnificent dinner tables, candelabras and warm overflowing elegance. Although this had the image of being a celebration for my lifetime, I knew it was a much more expanded happening than that. This was actually a celebration for each and every soul present.

From this side, you have the instant recognition of how all lives fit together and each person plays their part in making the whole of creation work. I fully recognized what a terrific and magical choice I had made during that lifetime. What an honor to bring so many people together with creative visions and the resources to make it all happen!

So the life review.

How natural it was for me to be directed to a movie theater. No popcorn.

My personal "movie" actually started with scenes that occurred before I was born. I saw how my parent's lives influenced the path to my destiny. Everyone was in the right place at the right time to inspire dreams, artistic ability and magical visions. There were fast scenes of railroads, pencil drawings and a quick "dot to dot" blueprints of connections to all the people who had the effect of inspiration on me during my youth and on through life.

I was shown the how's and why's of our family's moving from one location to another and how each of those moves placed me in the exact energetic position I needed to be in for the future. I saw how times of disappointment were actually opportunities to push me on to another location or into meeting other people. What seems to us, in life, to be problems or challenges or failures actually guide us into more suitable situations.

The hardest part was going through the reviews where I now understood I had disappointed others. I also saw how this pushed each of us to more perfected creations in the long run.

During those times, I asked for forgiveness but it had already been given. There was no reason to turn back. I watched as those thoughts just drifted off and disappeared into the ethers. With a little "ping," they were gone.

My thoughts turned to joy and childlike wonder at the number of creative people, all contracted to come together, in an exchange of energy that allowed us to dream in the wonderment of inspiration and freedom to create.

Awesome opportunity. Awesome opportunity.

The lesson here is that these awesome opportunities are available to each and every soul.

Dreams. Inspiration. Joy. That is what life is all about.

Learning to allow yourself to expand in the energy of joy. To allow inspiration to be the driving force of your life. Allow. Allow. Allow.

Is it time to increase your allowance? [laughing]

Faith is trusting the magic!

--Walt Disney

Pamela

I felt I had no personal connection to Walt Disney when I started, so I decided just to sit down and ask if he had anything to say and out he popped. For years I hadn't thought about his physical resemblance to my father until he reminded me, and yes, he did indeed look like him (the same mustache, similar haircut, that 50s-style debonair flair). Walt surprised me even further—with his connection to Aesop, the ancient Greek fabulist, as well as his take on George Orwell's novel Animal Farm were things that had never crossed my mind. And it's interesting that I had not read Carla's transmission of Walt's crossing over before I received my own transmission; both used metaphors of roller

*coasters and both incorporated the word "wonder" a lot. Walt
did have a sense of humor. The last line he transmitted to
me still cracks me up every time I read it. And he certainly
had a sparkle in his soul when he said it.*

Pamela
October 29, 2009

*Walt, do you have anything to comment about lessons
learned or life in heaven?*

Walt: Well, it's been a rollercoaster of activity and ingenuity.
I love color, lights, sound, drama. Animation is a world
reflective of nature and yet beyond. To have my hands in
every aspect of the work was thrilling. It was a little bit like
playing god, to make worlds that you can control so well, so
intimately. Having my hands in everything, tasting every
soup—that's what I loved.

Yes, I do realize I look a little like your father. I cultivated that
look, actually. I liked to look like everybody's father. Because
the characters we built and produced were part of your
family. That's how we saw it. We wanted to go into every
home in the nation, in the world, wherever we could, and
create an alternate reality. We didn't call it that at that time,
but we were able to have fun, express themes, play with
gender and animal roles in a way you could not do if people,
real human characters, were involved. We slipped in tiny
slights or political comments, though they were not obvious.

I did have a complex of ruling the world.

The success was not without drawbacks. I found family life
less than soothing. Even though I wanted a big family. I
tended to hide behind the bigness of things.

Mickey Mouse was everyman. He had a little bit of me in him. He wanted to put his arms around the world. He had his woman. He had his friends, even though they were a bit kooky and had faults. Blubbering ducks. Sneaky dogs. Foolish hens. George Orwell picked up the animated characters and made them serious, made them real in his novel *Animal Farm*. I am sure he was influenced by the Disney clan.

What's enduring about Walt Disney? I lived through these characters. We put heart in the story. We wanted to touch the imagination and glee of childhood. We felt there was a world of imagination to trigger in children. I best loved it when children would go to watch movies with their parents, with the entire family. A family movie that could be shared was intensely personal to me.

Many families thank me over here. I love to see eyes light up still. The wonder of it.

I traded in awe and wonder.

I had a great deal of connection to Aesop's Fables. In fact I feel I was Aesop, reincarnatedly speaking. The idea of using animals as allegory—we just took it as far as we could technically at that time in the 20th century.

What brings joy to the human race? This question, this query—socially, intellectually, emotionally, spiritually— should never, never be lost. Should never be forgotten or piled under heaps of everyday pressures, disasters, economic fallout. Even in the worst of times, don't let the children lose their sense of awe and wonder. It is that which keeps the human spirit alive. Let a puppet be your guide out of misery. If you can laugh, you will be saved.

That's my motto, even here.

If you can laugh at yourself, through the machinations of a duck, well, then, you're one step higher on the ladder of evolution.

--Walt Disney

"I love to see their eyes light up . . ."

JOHN LENNON

Musician/Visionary/Member of The Beatles

Born: October 9, 1940

Died: December 8, 1980

First Transmission: October 29, 2009

Carla

It's strange how these messages come in. Although there are sometimes visual images, the majority of the message for me comes much like downloading files into the computer. I'm the computer. The person on the other side is sending files and attachments. Most of the time, I know when there is "incoming."

John Lennon came in while I was out raking leaves. The fall colors were so pretty and he was enjoying them too. I think he was also enjoying that it wasn't his physical responsibility to rake up the leaves, but the action could be looked at as a meditation.

Rake. Rake. Rake. "If you can imagine it, you can establish it."

Rake. Rake. Rake. "If you can imagine it, you can establish it."

I've often heard the metaphysical phrase "If you can believe it, you can achieve it." But in this case, John was very specific about two of the words: imagine and establish. The word "imagine" is easily related to him but his emphasis on the word "establish" had even more impact or power behind it. As though he were trying to really impress this word on my mind.

So the raking was done for the day, and even though I tried to turn my focus toward him that night, it just wasn't happening. I kept thinking—let things simmer until done. Let things simmer until done so that you don't "get in the way" of it all.

And there I was—the next morning. Had John completed his download? Was my computer hung up? Where were we going here? It was time to check in.

His essence was very light—bordering on humorous. It felt like he was laughing at himself now that he was completely free of any physical body.

Carla
October 30, 2009

Tell me about crossing over. The feelings. The sights. The sounds. . .all of it.

John Lennon: You know about the times of drugs, spiritual seeking and meditation during my life. That whole search was about trying to get back to the essence of life on this side.

My crossing was swift, like stepping from black to white. One second I'm on the earth side of things. Next second I'm grounded on the other side. There was hardly any feeling of passage. Here. There. Done.

So does that mean I had achieved all that I'd wanted to while in body? No. It was just that when your time is over, it's over.

You can sometimes expand the time allotted on earth if desired. In my case, it wasn't desired. Sure, there was the possibility of creating so much more, but the creative point of inspiration had gotten so dark (with such a heavy feeling of responsibility) to me that the spark of joy was gone. Once that happens, you're out of your element—literally—and pushing against inspiration energetically.

So the crossing was fast and easy. The landing held no concerts, no mass crowds, no screaming fans, nothing but peace. You've watched in movies a scene where the person is standing in a certain place while the camera swirls around them?

That's the vision I had. I was standing on the most beautiful, sparkling ground. Everything was energy in motion with life far beyond perception.

The visions that swirled around me were extensive in size and wonder. Beautiful sparkling mountains changed to wide, sparkling oceans, which changed to emerald islands and snow-covered land. The turning visions continued with scenes of castles, then small dark London pubs. I was starting to think this is an all-inclusive resort. Which it is.

I soon found myself joined by another spirit or companion soul. The feeling of reuniting with a long-lost friend ran through my being. We actually didn't need to say anything to each other. I use the word "say," but everything here is actually done by mere thought.

The sense of peace that I had so longed for in life was now an actuality. No more seeking. No more search.

Home. I was home.

I believe that the constant search I traveled through in life came from a knowing that I had to get back home—and fast. The strange thing is—I was seeking something that I already possessed. I had just been looking for the porthole to it, which is naturally held inside us all.

The whole drug culture is one of two things: an escape from (and giving up responsibility to) reality because we aren't living up to our spiritual essence or trying to escape back into and living from our true spiritual essence. Either way, it's a search for a place that you already possess. All you have to do is connect with it—consciously.

Life on this side is peaceful. I don't have anything to create. I don't have any time limits. I don't feel any pressure to accomplish anything.

I do, however, still hold many connections to the earth plane through offering energetic inspiration or re-establishing inspiration already existing in the earth's consciousness.

This is done easily by flowing energy to songs or creations that already have a presence on your side. If you hear the song "Imagine" at a time that pops a spark of inspiration—I'm there. If you hear any song by the Beatles or have a phrase from a song that runs through your mind—I'm there.

We were quite a creative group [*the Beatles*]. How lucky we were to establish the things we were capable of creating. Our popularity was as much a whirlwind as our changing source of creation was. I sometimes didn't know whether to stop and enjoy the process or to try to run from it. But as a collective, we completed what we agreed to do. We were a family within a family of man. Most people don't get to experience that to the degree we did.

So, back to the phrase you kept hearing yesterday and my emphasis on the word **establish**. (*If you can imagine it, you can establish it.*)

How is the word "establish" energetically different from the word "achieve"? And how is the word "imagine" energetically different from the word "believe"?

It's only a slight difference in the source of original energy.

To believe is to know it is possible. To imagine is to open up to **all** possibility without limits. So, a belief is a limitation in a way of thought and creativity. A belief follows a pattern that has, most likely, not been set by yourself. To imagine is to open up to possibilities without limitation.

Energetically, "imagining" can spread much further and wider than anything you believe.

Establish. If one is achieving something, it is "set" with a specific goal from the get-go. Do you see the limitation on this?

Achievement often comes with giving away your power to others, in that they must deem your achievement as worthy. Although you can set personal goals of achievement through your previous experiences, those achievements have limitations.

On the other hand, "to establish" is to start, begin or launch something. Do you see how that leaves the accomplishment as unlimited, allowing space for further growth and success beyond belief or vision?

It's unlimited possibility. Unlimited points of completion. Infinity.

No matter who the individual is, there is room for them to establish themselves on the earth plane by conscious connection with their soul.

No matter who the individual is, their life is important as part of the whole.

No matter who the individual is, there is space created for their imagination to bring expanding thought or joy or sorrow or peace.

Consciously establish your highest dreams and leave room open for that establishment to grow into infinity.

--John Lennon

* * *

Pamela

After seeing the Michael Jackson movie "This Is It," I went to sleep with John Lennon on my mind as I knew he would be our last interviewee. That night I dreamed I was with Michael; when I woke, however, I heard John saying three words to me— "Reeducate. Reorganize. Reinvigorate."— and I sensed he would finish this book with an awesome planetary vision. Remaining in bed, I typed my transmission out just as it came, in the dark with my laptop on my stomach. In contrast to others, John had a halting energy as if he continually returned to silence to re-gather his thoughts. Within his silence and throughout his words, I could feel the deep longing he held inside his soul for planetary peace, to the point that it made me burst into tears. Throughout his transmission John shied away from speaking personally about his life; it wasn't his goal or compelling vision. He is, simply, a vision-bringer, and he seems to touch the world at the very point of its loneliness, as if the lyric, "where do all the lonely people come from," was the very question which had ignited his search for higher truth. That song, "Eleanor Rigby," and John's connection to the Beatles, especially to his fellow Beatle Paul McCartney, still vibrates strongly through the realms, but it took a little research to fully explain why. (More about that in my Epilogue.)

Finally, days after I had transcribed the group's "Parting Words," it occurred to me that although the lineup had gathered to speak in one voice, they had somehow chosen John to be their mouthpiece. As he stood out in front of them, a vehicle of light and focus, they used his gifts of metaphor and succinctness to communicate their deepest final feelings. It was an indelible image. Even in Heaven, John Lennon remains at once an individual and a cosmos.

John, is there anything you'd like to express?

John: There is an urgent need to reeducate the world.

Everything we have been taught, everything we have been blindsided to in our upbringing, is not true. We are not limited beings. We are not who we think we are.

YOU—are not who you think you are.

The Beatles brought such a crushing momentum to the world because there were parts in all of us that were essentially free. We held this vision. We pursued this vision. We saw the power four people could have and we dove into the meaning of that. We knew that which would free us would free the world. We were not just a pop group. We were not just a rock group. We were a band of free men leading a world to a different consciousness. It had to come in the way it did because those was the times. In these times, things like this—this book, other movements—these are the bands leading people to higher consciousness.

Heed the call.

Dark must become white. There is no other way to say it. What is hidden must be revealed. What is closed must be opened. What is rejected must be embraced. A starving child must become beautiful in our eyes so that we will embrace it. An abused mother calls for us to put our arm around her, not shun her, not walk away. A homeless person must call out to our compassion, not our ignorance. We must open our eyes and see in a new way.

This is the call of this generation, to wash our eyes out with a new kind of compassion. Sometimes I feel it's the worst of times and yet I also see the brilliance of a future where all men and women shall rest in the bosom of light and love. I don't mean to sound sappy. I trust that the light will do its work and find renewal in the hearts of every man and woman and child. It is not only in the children where we must find hope. That child is inside all of us.

I sought this in my life but I had to sequester myself from society eventually to hear that voice. We can so easily be confused by all the patterning that society throws at us, not the least which is the media. The media needs to wake up that they are creating patterns of thoughts—greed, lack of verisimilitude, dishonesty—and that like attracts like. They will find themselves in a cesspool of deceit and greed. This desire to make money for its own sake must be changed. It is sick, truly.

The money I had meant nothing to me, truly. But it can be binding. I longed to lead a simple life.

John seems to have a need to stop and think, and then reboot. Long spaces of silence in between the transmission. Let's sit in the silence, *he would seem to say as if he wanted us to meditate together. Then he'd start again.*

Reeducation. Reorganization. Renewal. Imagine that as a political platform, a leader who actually has the power and the insight to lead the globe through massive transformation of the spirit, one who has gone through transformation him or herself, who stands up and says, *Yes, this is the way the new reality is. I've been there and seen the light.* Maybe it will take someone who has had a near-death experience, a walk-in, a spirit from another being-realm more advanced than the common man but dear in heart, determined in vision, belonging to the human race and yet above its frailties and greed and defaults.

"All the lonely people, where do they all come from?" A haunting song Paul and I wrote. We were feeling this undercurrent in life, this quiet desperation that leads to self-destruction. From this vantage point, we see how truly wasteful that loneliness is, how necessary it is that people join together, to recognize how to say "I love you" to each other, to look behind the facades and pick someone up off the sidewalk, take them in, feed them, care for them. We are family. We are one.

We are not separate beings on an island. How I wish I could convey the words, the rhythm, the harmony, to express that and have it lodge in your heart as a guiding star.

How deeply do I wish that.

How deeply do I wish that for you.

My heart opens to this vision and light streams forth to touch each and every one of you, to ignite within you the dream this soul has held for eons. Light your fire now. The world is coming in a flash, in a torrent, in an avalanche to pick you up and demand your best.

Reeducate. Reorganize. Renew.

There is a massive need for reorganization. The money system. The distribution of supplies. The way men and women interact. The way families interact within themselves and with each other. There is a greater vision of family interaction, communal living, communal assistance, not one family inside a home with closed doors. We can care about each other beyond our closed doors.

Whatever I could say about my private life now is not important. What I have to give is this vision.

Hand in hand. Heart to heart. Head to head.

The life we have now is ours to give.

--John Lennon

"If you can imagine it, you can establish it."

PARTING WORDS

Pamela
November 9, 2009

I asked one last time if there was anything anybody wanted to say or that we needed to add to the book. It seemed the group replied as a whole, and this is how they wanted the book to end:

The Group: If there is a positive aspect to this book, it is that we could all sit down and *feast*, so to speak, at the table together. For this reason, we are delighted to be in a book of this sort, to present our deepest desires and insights. Our lives, as famous as they were, were not about accomplishments—that is, it was not the accomplishments that lingered in the soul; but rather, it was that point of contact, human to human, heart to heart, that lights the soul chain between us.

If you, Humanity, could look out onto yourselves and see the chain of existence, the web of lights, the destiny of souls, the sacrament of being, then there would be no wars, no poverty, no hunger, no lack. The web would find itself full of everything it needed.

Take our eyes from heaven and look down upon yourselves, *as we see you.*

It is, truly, the heaven on earth to behold.

--The Group

EPILOGUE – Carla

What can I say? This has been an awesome adventure. Here are a few afterthoughts, from my perspective, on each of the Souls involved.

There was a distinct energetic feeling from each of our subjects as they communicated with us. The energy was probably similar to their personalities in life, but there was also a supernaturally free feeling to each person. It was a clear, fresh and open essence without negative undertones of any kind.

Walter Cronkite:
Walter Cronkite had the deep, grounded and humorous feeling of wisdom. He is happy where he is but one could also feel that he would love to have a chance to take over that anchor seat again. I think he loved his work and he loved his life. He had a respect for real news without an overlying opinion. And he thinks that some things were better in the good old days.
He is the essence of honesty and integrity. A wonderful example of respect for one's self. I think he wanted us each to know that we all have that quality in us. It's part of our birthright.

Michael Jackson:
Michael Jackson is pure talent. His energy felt so excited (almost impatient) about future possibilities. I have no doubt that he is spreading his influence not only to those he knew in this lifetime but also to any soul interested in the arts of music and entertainment. Michael may end up being a bigger influence after his death than he was while alive. That's a huge statement to make considering his present accomplishments. Even now, he's saying, "Call on me. I'll be there."

Abraham Lincoln:
Abraham Lincoln. What a presence he is! I could actually feel the relief about the completion of his life's destiny. The depth of his soul left me with a feeling that he had chosen many lifetimes of responsibility before that lifetime. Responsibility was not a lesson he needed to learn in any new lifetime, but rather a task he could accept and complete without hesitation. He understands the importance of a Divine Plan and the knowing that there is more to life than what we perceive.

Albert Einstein:
Albert Einstein had the feeling of mind in constant motion. And, that's where he preferred to be—in constant motion. He has so much more to communicate and I'm sure we haven't heard the last from him—not by a long shot!

One could **feel** his soul's ingrained love of numbers and equations and how they all fit into the scheme of life throughout eternity.

If Michael Jackson's soul was filled with music and dance, Albert Einstein's soul is filled with the talent of math and science—pure math and science that leaves the door open to Divine Influence.

Amelia Earhart:
Amelia Earhart's energy felt as if it flowed on a calm stream. When Amelia was explaining her crossing, she wasn't necessarily talking about how her infamous last flight ended. I do believe that she must have left her body before the plane went down since that's the way she explained it. However, that doesn't mean that she died at the end of that flight.
It felt like I was experiencing the end of that flight along with her as it was happening. I do think her spirit took "flight" before the plane went down. In the cockpit, she must have been doing the automatic, physically required actions

necessary to try to save the plane, but I don't think she was consciously "in body" as it was happening. Her explanation had an "out-of-body" sensation to it.

This book has made me realize that there are wide possibilities to the way we cross over. Not just a tunnel. Not just floating toward a bright light.

Each crossing is personal and varied.

In Amelia's case, it was a surprise to hear the explanation of her crossing through a water-based experience rather than a flying experience. She gave me the impression that, for her, the experience of coming into the physical world and leaving the physical world were comparable to leaving the womb at birth and returning to the womb at death. I think this is what made this book experience so interesting for me. It didn't follow normal thought and belief.

The explanation of her crossing doesn't mean that her life ended in the ocean—although that is a real possibility. She left me with the impression that the answers to her demise will be discovered soon but they weren't mine to find.

Paul Newman:
Paul Newman still has "it", no matter how you define "it". His soul carries what could be the dictionary's definition of charisma.
It's hard to explain in words but there was a feeling of swagger without an ego attachment to it. I think he wanted to say more about how things happen for a good reason—even if there are hard emotional qualities attached to the experiences. It was as though he wanted to show me building blocks and how each block adds to, but also sets, a foundation for any event.

One thing for sure, Paul was still having fun in the afterlife with all of his movie buddies and appreciated the chance to have the opportunities and influence in physical life that he had.

Walt Disney:
Walt Disney was a purely delightful experience for me. He so loves creating universes within universes with no boundaries to the possibilities available. I felt that he must still watch over the Disney productions like a mother hen. Not for fear of too much expansion but rather because he doesn't want the quality of magic to be diluted in any way. If that's true, I think he's doing a good job of it.
Disney brought magic to life through whatever creation, invention or work was necessary to get it done. It reminds me of the work that NASA does but for a totally different purpose.

Faith is trusting the magic.

With that thought, he gave me the knowing that we are never given a dream without also being given the components necessary to bring that dream to life. What an awesome thing that is to know!

John Lennon:
And as for our final guest in the book, John Lennon, his soul felt deeper than most gave him credit for when alive. It was as though his soul structure was part music and part Gandhi. I have no doubt that, even today, his influence is felt all over the world. It's almost as though he and Bono are brothers in soul structure with their similar activities in music and world vision.
His words explaining the quantum difference between the words "believe" and "imagine" along with "achieve" and "establish" made a huge impact on me. I still think about those words before I go to sleep at night.

Einstein said imagination is more important than knowledge.

Disney knew that imagination led to establishing by making magical universes a physical reality.

If we truly understand this to be true, what can you establish through *your* imagination?

--Carla

EPILOGUE - Pamela

In the midst of finishing this book I uncovered notes I had typed to myself back in 1999. Apparently Carla and I have known each other for at least that long because I found I'd written down something she'd said.

It was just one word. "Synchrodestiny."

I'd never heard that word before. Ten years later, it seems to be the exact description of what this project has been all about.

Surely, it was synchrodestiny that brought Carla and I together. And it was definitely synchrodestiny that allowed our subjects to meet *us*.

How to define it? It's a big idea, but I'll try.

Synchrodestiny is the web of existence, the moments in time that take us out of time. It's a reflection of the interconnectedness of all being that allows the seeming barriers between the realms to dissolve and cosmic coincidence to occur. Synchrodestiny allows us to know more than we think we do, to be in the exact space and time of another. We experience synchrodestiny in chance encounters that change our life (and aren't "chance" at all), in the ability to hear another's soul longings, in the power of love to transcend physical limitations and penetrate impossibility.

It's no wonder we become thrilled when we experience signs of it.

And the experience of this book has been inundated with such signs.

The rational brain is fascinated by facts it can prove. So, at this point, it's probably worth reiterating that Carla and I did no prior research on our subjects before channeling them. We did do a little bit *after* the fact, and what we found bedazzled the mind.

Sometimes it was small things. For instance, Abraham Lincoln used the word "mountebanks" to describe family lineages which were destined to lead but which had squandered their power. I hesitated for a moment when I initially received the word because I didn't know its meaning. Later I checked a dictionary and found that "mountebank" was the perfect word for the context; it means "charlatan," and was a word clearly used more in those times than today. In fact I found several instances in historical documents where Lincoln himself had been called a mountebank by his own opponents.[2]

As I looked deeper into history, more synchronicities were revealed. In my transmission with Lincoln he talked about how he felt he was putting on his white gloves "for the last time" before going to the Ford's Theater the night he was assassinated. I had no idea this was true, but later, research revealed that Lincoln was indeed wearing white gloves the night John Wilkes Booth shot him to death in that theater; in fact the blood-stained gloves are now on view at the Abraham Lincoln Presidential Library and Museum in Springfield, Illinois., as part of the Taper Collection. You can even see a photo of them online.[3]

---

[2] *The Lincoln Log: A Daily Chronology of the Life of Abraham Lincoln* incorporates Lincoln Day-by-Day: A Chronology, compiled by the Lincoln Sesquicentennial Commission with the cooperation and support of the Abraham Lincoln Association and published by the Government Printing Office in 1960. See online: http://www.thelincolnlog.org/view/1844/2/16

[3] See this website for a picture of the gloves: [http://www.msnbc.msn.com/id/19296386/displaymode/1176/

And the feelings of dread Lincoln said he'd been experiencing? Unbeknownst to me, history had already recorded that in the months prior to his assassination he had had several "eerie" precognitive experiences of impending doom. In the year before his death, there was a well-documented moment when he had seen his double in a mirror, with one of the figures eerily fading. And just ten days before his assassination Lincoln recorded in his journal a dream in which he saw mourners sobbing around a catafalque in the East Room. When he asked the dream figures who had died, they replied, "The President." And it wasn't a one-time dream; on the day of the death, he told his bodyguard he'd had a similar dream three nights in a row. As a consequence, the bodyguard begged him not to go to the theater but Lincoln replied he had already promised his wife. And when Lincoln finally did leave for the theater, he gave the bodyguard not his customary salutation of "Good night," but rather a strangely prophetic "Good bye." Later, when the bodyguard heard about the shooting, he commented that his mind immediately returned to that uncanny moment of parting—as if Lincoln had *known* it was indeed his final time.

None of this I knew until researched after the fact.

Even seeming contradictions between our various transmissions led us through research to a deeper understanding. For instance, when I read over Carla's transmission of Lincoln, I noticed it talked of a funeral train (she says she "saw" Lincoln looking out over the train), and yet Lincoln had talked with me about seeing his *caisson*. A little delving into history proved both were true. A train did take Lincoln's body from Washington D.C. to Springfield, Illinois, for internment via a circuitous route through New York. But prior to that, following his funeral, his body was taken in a *caisson* from the White House up Pennsylvania Avenue to the Capital, where it laid in state until it was taken to the depot of the Baltimore and Ohio Railroad for final burial in Illinois. I found these facts online, in a moving review of Lincoln's funeral day, published in the May 6, 1865 edition of the popular magazine *Harper's Weekly* [4]. (It's worth checking out, if only for the intimate details of this historic funeral ceremony.)

But I was still wondering why Lincoln had mentioned to Carla about his after-death reunion with his son Willie? After all, he'd had several children who died before him. But research revealed that Willie, his third son, had indeed been Lincoln's favorite. Apparently afflicted with typhoid, Willie died in 1862 at the tender age of eleven (three years before Lincoln), and it's been recorded that Lincoln had been devastated by his death. During Carla's transmission, she recalls seeing a vision of young Willie overlaid on Lincoln's funeral train but hadn't known why. Further research revealed that after Lincoln's death Willie's casket had been removed from its original resting place and placed on the Lincoln funeral train back to Illinois, where on May 4,1865, it was situated beside his father's casket in a common tomb at Oak Ridge Cemetery.

Such is the mystery—and metaphor—of expanded vision.

Still, Carla and I kept wondering why Abe had insinuated himself into our lineup when everyone else seemed to belong to modern times. In fact, my original subtitle for this book had been "Channeled Interviews with the Illuminated Souls *of Our Time*," but Lincoln's self-inclusion nixed that idea. But afterwards, I discovered that Lincoln and his wife had been deeply fascinated by spiritualism and they had even attended séances in the White House, conducted by two lady mediums who had tried to contact their son Willie. One such medium, Miss Nettie Colburn Maynard, even later published a short book of her recollections, which had fallen

---

[4] Find the article at: http://www.sonofthesouth.net/leefoundation/civil-war/1865/April/abraham-lincoln-funeral.htm

out of print but is now miraculously available online.[5] Her counseling, done in full trance, seems have included advice about major military maneuvers during the Civil War, some of which Lincoln is even said to have followed!

But the spiritualist fixation that surrounded Lincoln did not end with his death. Indeed a number of presidential family members and guests over the years have reported seeing visions of Lincoln's ghost in the White House or, at the very least, felt his *presence*—among them, Eleanor Roosevelt, Jacqueline Kennedy Onassis, Calvin Coolidge's wife, the poet Carl Sandburg, and even Queen Wilhelmina of The Netherlands. The latter, a guest of FDR's, claimed she heard footsteps one night, then knocking, and when she opened her bedroom door, she saw Lincoln in the hallway dressed in a top hat! (Well, she was staying in the Lincoln bedroom after all!)

And yet, despite the fun of these stories (and there are many more you can find in history books and online), neither Carla nor I ever felt we were communicating with Lincoln's ghost; rather, as with all of our subjects, we felt we were channeling...their *souls*. And yet could the seeds of Lincoln's appearance in our book have been planted long ago, before we ever met him in 2009? A hint might be detected in the following passage I came upon in that same *Harper's Weekly* funeral report mentioned above—in words written by a journalist who was clearly (if unusually) attuned to the spiritual realms:

> "Is WASHINGTON dead? Is DAVID dead? Is any
> man that was ever fit to live dead?? Disenthralled
> of flesh, risen to the unobstructed sphere where
> passion never comes, he [Lincoln] begins his

---

[5] The book, published in 1917, is titled *Was Abraham Lincoln a Spiritualist?* It can be downloaded free of charge from this website: http://www.ghostcircle.com/_ebooks.html

---

illimitable work. His life is now grafted upon
the infinite, and will be fruitful, as no earthly
life can be."

My goodness: "*Illimitable work…grafted upon the infinite.*"
And that was what passed as journalism in 1865!

Yes, indeed, Mr. Lincoln!

* * *

And then there was Walt Disney! I am still wondering, was it
heavenly intention or merely human mistake that made me
mix up George Orwell's novels *Animal Farm* and *1984*? To
backtrack a bit: when Walt was saying that Disney's animal
characters must have influenced one of Orwell's novels, I
thought I "heard" him say *1984,* although I knew he was
referring to Orwell's novel about animals (which, of course, is
titled *Animal Farm).* The title was left incorrect in the
manuscript, however, until I went to confirm the years Orwell
had published both novels, at which point I discovered two
things: Not only could Orwell have been truly influenced by
Disney characters (they were well in the public eye by the
time his novels were published), but the novel *1984* was
actually made into a movie by the Disney company during
the sixties (although to less than stellar success). Why these
facts overlaid themselves in my mind, I really can't say, but
perhaps it's a reflection of the way cosmic mind works…or
maybe it was just Walt's way of killing two facts with one
stone!

***

Beatle John Lennon also proved to be a powerful son of
synchrodestiny. When I transcribed John's line that referred
to the song "Eleanor Rigby"—*"the song Paul and I wrote"*—I
was jarred for a moment. I wasn't at all certain that Paul
McCartney and John Lennon had *both* written "Eleanor

Rigby," although it seemed reasonable enough—they had collaborated on so many songs, why not this one? Searching the web for clarification, I found a fascinating discussion on Wikipedia[6] which suggested the song was mainly written by Paul McCartney but that all the Beatles contributed, as did their friend Paul Shotten. I was wondering, then, why John would claim so much authorship until later in the article I came across this intriguing line from the book *All We Are Saying: The Last Major Interview with John Lennon and Yoko Ono*.

The author, David Sheff writes:

> Lennon recalled in 1980 that "'Eleanor Rigby' was Paul's baby, and I [Lennon] helped with the education of the child...."

Clearly, back then, John *felt* he'd taken a major role in the creation of the song, and apparently, from my transmission, he still felt the same way! But the quote also illuminated something else very important—reflected in the way John used the word "education." Indeed, that was the very theme of his transmission to me—that what the world most needed at this critical juncture was a firm *re-education*.

Reeducate. Reorganize. Renew.

***

But it was with Michael Jackson that synchrodestiny came to a head—for both Carla and myself. Michael's energy was so strong and so creative that it was bound to bleed over into our daily lives. Through the writing of this book, Carla would often comment that she felt Michael "wasn't done yet," and

---

[6] See "Eleanor Rigby" on Wikipedia online: http://en.wikipedia.org/wiki/Eleanor_Rigby

one day she announced she had received new lyrics to "Human Nature," a song from his best-selling album *Thriller*. At the time I didn't pay much attention because I was involved in other things and, honestly, didn't even recognize the name of the song; on the other hand, I was more than a little bit peeved that Michael wasn't giving *me* lyrics. After all, I was the musician and aspiring librettist!

Then one night, on the way to attend theater in Manhattan, I had the energetic experience that was briefly alluded to on page 43. After having taken the wrong subway, I was caught in a drizzle and had to walk a considerable number of blocks in the rain. Instead of cursing the situation, I found myself humming a phrase from one of Michael's songs over and over again—a song whose title I didn't even know. Suddenly feeling uninhibited, I started scatting the melody, then burst out into dance, including posing in that Michael Jackson freeze-stop sort of way. The more I sang, the freer I felt, the happier I got, as if the great rhythm of life was streaming through me—right there on Eighth Street in Greenwich Village. It was a powerful moment, if rather hilarious. And a few days later, when I finally wrote down the experience, the transmission that ends Michael's chapter came flowing through me.

But that was not the last of Michael.

The day I finished his last transmission, I went alone in the evening to see the film *This is It*—the documentary of Michael's last concert tour, abruptly terminated by his death. Even though I had always admired Michael's talent, I was not a rabid fan, yet now, watching the film, I became very, very emotional; in fact, it felt "energetically" as if Michael were sitting in the seat next to me, holding my hand. And then suddenly—it must have been the third song or so—I heard those ten little notes I had been singing in the rain. Not only that, Michael was singing the song *in the same mood* that had come to me in the street—very laid-back—and using *the same gestures* (more or less—as close as I, in my pathetic attempt, could come). Afterwards, I went online to find the name of the song using the only words I could remember: "why, why." The song, I soon discovered, was "Human Nature" by Steve Pocaro and John Bettis, and the lyrics referred to someone walking through the streets of New York City ("The Big Apple")—at night!

The very song whose lyrics Carla had channeled earlier from Michael.

But he still hadn't given me any lyrics!

And then, a few nights later, I felt compelled to go to bed early and awoke around one in the morning with a strong inner urge to seek out "Human Nature" on YouTube. Intrigued, I watched Michael perform the song and then went to find the lyrics online. I can't say that what happened next could be called "channeling" because it did not flow fast and furiously; rather, I strongly felt Michael's presence guiding me to understand how to write a song—pointing out the different cadences, the various vowel sounds, the hooks, even the storyline of the original lyrics. It was like having the best songwriting teacher in the world—right at my shoulder. Over the next few days I/we did a lot of tweaking, but finally a complete new set of lyrics arrived—an event that somehow gave me enormous joy. Because the experience had a different feel from that of the transmissions, I tend to think of these lyrics as more a "collaboration" than a channeling. Nevertheless, at the heart of the song remains Michael's very personal message—straight from Heaven.

One day I/we hope somebody, somewhere, will record it.

***

There are many more stories *in between the lines* of *Heaven*

Speaks, but in the end, while facts can fuel the mind, it is sentiment that serves the soul. These facts and synchronicities, final impressions and afterthoughts, have all been offered only to lead you back to the real message of this book—*that life is eternal, love is immortal, and death is just a horizon.*

And with that in mind, and with our deepest gratitude to the original songwriters (and of course, the *original performer!*), we would like to close this book with the two new sets of lyrics we received for "Human Nature." Indeed, this entire book might be seen as a new and revised version of what it truly means to have a "human nature" and how we might live and breathe, dance and sing, on a stage that is bigger and more glorious than we have ever imagined possible.

For Carla and myself, it's been a wonderful and awe-filled ride.

--Pamela Bloom

"Human Nature/Soul Connection"
--Michael and Pamela
November 2, 2009

Looking out
Across the blue-kissed sky
Heaven blinks an open eye
Hear my voice
No longer shy
It's Love reminding you

If it's true
We're more than strangers
For once don't hold yourself back
If our love
Is just an open door
Then let me fly right through

If they say why why
Tell em it's our soul connection
Why why
Come on, jes do me this way
If they ask why why
Tell em it's our soul connection
Why, why not love me this way

I like lovin this way
I like livin this way
I like givin this way

Heaven's cool
New space and time
A place to find and make your rhyme
No judgment here
No prison walls
Where every dude (and girl) stands tall

If they say why why
Tell em it's your soul connection
Aye, aye
Come on, let's do it this way
If they say why why
Tell em it's our new direction
Aye, aye, let's live it this way

We look down
Across your town
And see the "you" that you hide
Let it go
Those old familiars
And be the jewel inside

If they say why why
Tell em it's your soul connection
Aye, aye
Come on, let's do it this way
If they say why why
Tell em it's our new direction
Aye, aye, let's live it this way

If they say why why
Tell em it's your soul connection
Aye, aye
Come on, let's do it this way
If they say why why
Tell em it's divine protection
Aye, aye let's live it this way

I like lovin this way
I like livin this way
I like givin this way

"Human Nature"
--Michael and Carla
October 20, 2009

Looking out
On life's vast ocean
Endless movement everywhere
Hear the voice
That moves my spirit
It's open if I dare.

Take me out
Into the heartbeat
No stopping this delight
The chance for love
Is always waiting
I'm grabbing it tonight.

If they say
Why Why
Tell them that it's human nature
Why Why Can't we do it that way
If they say
Why Why
Tell them it's true human nature
Why Why Don't we do it that way

Reaching out
To touch a Stranger
Feel the light that's in their Soul
We are One
No separation
For Love is always there

If they say
Why Why
Tell them that it's human nature

Why Why Can't we do it that way
If they say
Why Why
Tell them it's true human nature
Why Why Don't we do it that way

I like livin that way
I like lovin that way

Looking out
On Love's vast ocean
Watch how
Lives begin to change
One by one
Compassion Emotion
Let Love just lead the way

If they say
Why Why
Tell them that it's human nature
Why Why Can't we do it that way
If they say
Why Why
Tell them it's true human nature
Why Why Don't we do it that way

***

BIOS

HEAVEN SPEAKS is a joint project of two conscious mediums, Pamela Bloom and Carla Flack.

Pamela Bloom

PAMELA BLOOM is an award-winning writer, interfaith minister and intuitive counselor/healer whose passion for spiritual exploration has taken her through many disciplines, including Judaism, Tibetan Buddhism, Western mysticism, energy healing and the Divine Feminine.

An intuitive opening around the age of thirty inspired her to develop a unique form of energy healing that combined clairvoyant insight with the medium of her singing voice. During the early nineties she honed this skill as a counselor on staff at the Manhattan Center for Living, founded by Marianne Williamson to assist those with life-challenging illnesses. She is also a third-degree Reiki master and Johrei practitioner.

For over 25 years Pamela has also been a highly published writer in many fields. As a music critic she has been a Contributing Editor at top entertainment publications; as a travel writer she received the Lowell Thomas Travel Journalism Award twice for her guidebooks on Brazil. Her articles on a variety of lifestyle topics have appeared in the *New York Times, Los Angeles Times, Chicago Tribune, Village Voice, New York Post* and *Parabola, New Age Journal* and *Elle* magazine, among others. Her latest book is *The Power of Compassion: Stories that Open the Heart, Heal the Soul, and Change the World*, to be published by Hampton Roads, in April, 2010. Also new for 2010 is *The Little Guitarra Who Played Herself*, an award-winning fable for profound children, and her self-produced CD, titled *Buddha Heart: Chants for Love, Healing & Enlightenment*—all available at Amazon.com.

Enthralled with the power of creativity to move the soul, Pamela offers private sessions and workshops designed to trigger inspirational leaps of consciousness.

* * *

Carla Flack

CARLA FLACK has been an intuitive counselor and spiritual coach for over 35 years. Her client list includes celebrities, artists, authors, executives and ordinary people from all walks of life. Curiosity set her on a course of study through various esoteric arts such as astrology, numerology, meditation and expanding consciousness until she eventually settled into a focus on the two disciplines that held her interest the most: tarot and angels.

For years, Carla was a featured reader in AOL's Crystal Ball Room, which led to her being CEO of an independent internet website of highly praised intuitive counselors from around the world.

Over the past 20 years, Carla has been a published author of numerous articles, newsletters and books on a variety of metaphysical topics and continues her passionate journey into understanding consciousness and the soul's evolution.

She is the grandmother of two delightful earth angels, Reanna and Sierra, who are a constant source of wonder and inspiration.

BOOKS BY THE AUTHORS

•

PAMELA BLOOM

The Power of Compassion: Stories that Open the Heart, Heal the Soul and Change the World (Hampton Roads, 2010)

The Heart Sutra, Dalai Lama's Altar Kit (Bridgewater Books, 2002)

Buddhist Acts of Compassion (Conari Press, 2000)

Brazil Up Close (Hunter Publishing, 1997)

Amazon Up Close (Hunter Publishing, 1997)

On the Wings of Angels (Ariel Press, 1995)

Fielding's Amazon (Fielding's, 1995)

Fielding's Brazil (Fielding, 1993, 1995)

CARLA FLACK

Anyone Can Read Tarot Workbook (Angelight Publishing, 1986)

Tarot: The Halo Method (1st Books, 2002)

Prayers for Every Need, Volumes One and Two (Guideposts, 2000), Contributor

ACKNOWLEDGMENTS

A book such as *HEAVEN SPEAKS* spans the realms of existence, but it could not have been accomplished without the loving support and inspiration of earthly friends.

From Carla

This project could not have been completed without the years of support from my "meta" friends: Judy, Jan, Sarsa, Vickie, Radleigh, Janet, Randy, Trees, Kristy, Barbara, MaryEllen, Trudy, the AP Staff and all those not mentioned here (but you know who you are).

My appreciation also has to include my family: Tere, Bobette, Nikki, Misty, Reanna and Sierra. All of whom are a constant beam of inspiration (and sometimes irritation). I'm sending you prayers and angels and my deepest gratitude to all of you.

And to Ken, for saying just the right thing at just the right time in just the right place—this may not have been what you were thinking of when you made that statement but it sure has been a pleasure. . . and then some.

From Pamela

A lifetime of thanks and love to Faye Levey for her enthusiasm to read every chapter as it was written; an interdimensional kiss and hug to Alan DeValle, for mirroring who I am; a huge hug to Marcus Faber, Susan Kaplan and Rick Nichols for their early readings of the manuscript; a cosmic kiss to Iwona Drelich for her dedicated design support; to Earthgate for opening the portal; and gratitude without end to the late spiritual healer Mokichi Okada, whose admiration for the book *Gone West* by J.S.M. Ward, a pioneer undertaking in its day, must have surely triggered in me the passion to undertake a similar journey.

PHOTO CREDITS

WALTER CRONKITE
Page 13: At the 35th Apollo II Anniversary, July 20, 2004. Source: Wiki Commons. Public domain.
Page 28: On air, announcing the assassination of President John F. Kennedy, Jr., November 22, 1963, taken from television. Wiki Commons. Public domain.

MICHAEL JACKSON
Page 29: Circa 1993. ©Neal Preston/Corbis Images.
Page 45: Performing during the halftime show at the NFL's Super Bowl XXVII in Pasadena, California, 1993. ©Gary Hershorn/Reuters/Corbis Images.

ABRAHAM LINCOLN
Page 47: Taken two weeks after Lincoln's presidential nomination on June 3, 1860, in Springfield, IL. Photographer: Alexander Hessler. Wiki Commons. Public domain.
Page 58: The "Gettysburg Portrait." Taken on November 8th, 1863, two weeks before his Gettysburg Address. Photographer: Alexander Gard. Wiki Commons. Public domain.

ALBERT EINSTEIN
Page 59: During a lecture in Vienna in 1921 (age 42). Photographer: Ferdinand Schmutzer. Wiki Commons. Public domain.
Page 71: ©Ruth Orkin/Getty Images.

AMELIA EARHART
Page 73: Wiki Commons. Public domain.
Page 82: Steve Pitcairn Collection. The Lincoln Highway National Museum & Archives.

PAUL NEWMAN
Page 83: October, 1980. ©Douglas Kirkland/Corbis Images.
Page 90: Posing at his apartment on New York's Fifth Avenue Feb. 9, 1999, having just received good reviews for his supporting role in the new film "Message in a Bottle." AP Photo. ©Jim Cooper/New York Daily News.

WALT DISNEY
Page 91: ©Alfred Eisenstaedt. Time & Life Pictures. January 1, 1953. Getty Images.
Page 100: Wiki Commons. Public domain.

JOHN LENNON
Page 101: ©Michael Ochs. Michael Ochs Archives/Getty Images.
Page 111: Performing at the One To One Concert in Madison Square Garden, New York City, New York. 1972. ©Thomas, Monaster/New York Daily News.

Notes and Favorite Quotes

SOUL CONNECTIONS Unlimited is a publishing media firm dedicated to supporting projects that open the heart and heal the soul. To interest us in other projects, please e-mail:

Contact@SoulConnectionsUnlimited.com

For general press and publishing inquiries about HEAVEN SPEAKS, please e-mail:

Contact@HeavenSpeaksTheBook.com

To contact Carla Flack for personal intuitive sessions, workshops, interviews and book readings, please e-mail:

Carla@HeavenSpeaksTheBook.com

To contact Pamela Bloom for personal intuitive sessions, workshops, interviews and book readings, please e-mail:

Pamela@HeavenSpeaksTheBook.com

BLOG ALERT!

Check out our lively blog, author information and book excerpts at our new website below.

www.HeavenSpeaksTheBook.com

Plus join our mailing list for news, press kit, special gifts and more!

STAY TUNED!

On the schedule are upcoming volumes of HEAVEN SPEAKS!

Classic Hollywood: Bob Hope, Bogart, Tracy & others
The Rat Pack: Sinatra, Dean Martin, etc.
Great Artists. . . and more

To be continued...

TALK TO US!
We'd love to hear how HEAVEN SPEAKS has touched your life. Please feel free to contact us via e-mail or from our website: www.HeavenSpeakstheBook.com

May Heaven grace you with inspiration, joy, revelation and the synchronicity of Soul.

CPSIA information can be obtained at www.ICGtesting.com
Printed in the USA
LVOW13s1549101213

364712LV00003B/664/P